Shades and Flip-flops on
Zakynthos - 3rd Edition

Shades and Flip-flops on Zakynthos - 3rd Edition is a pictorial and descriptive journey through the history and beauty of the Greek paradise island of Zakynthos set in the blue Mediterranean sea. Visit its beaches, resorts and villages on this lovely island.

by Norfolk Watercolour Artist - Alan R. Massen
Published in Great Britain by Rainbow Publications UK

First Published in 2016 by Rainbow Publications UK
2nd Edition in 2019 by Rainbow Publications UK
3rd Edition in 2020 by Rainbow Publications UK

Copyright © 2020 Alan R. Massen

The moral right of Alan R. Massen to be identified as the author of this work has been asserted in accordance with the UK Copyright, Designs and Patents Act of 1988. All rights reserved. No part of this book may be reproduced, or stored in a retrieval system, or transmitted in any form or by any means, electronic, mechanical, photocopying, recording, or otherwise, without the prior written permission of both the author and the above publisher of this book All imagery and illustrations

© Alan R. Massen

Neither the publisher nor the author can accept liability for the use of any of the materials, methods or information recommended in this book or for any consequences arising out of their use, nor can they be held responsible for any errors or omissions that may be found in the text or may occur at a future date as a result of changes in rules, laws or equipment All manufacturers, sellers, product names and services identified in this book are used in editorial fashion and for the benefit of such companies with no intention of any infringement of trademarks. No such use or the use of any trade name is intended to convey endorsement or other affiliation with this book. Every effort has been made to obtain the necessary permissions with reference to copyright material, both illustrative and quoted. We apologize for any omissions in this respect and will be pleased to make the appropriate acknowledgements in any future edition.

Paperback Edition ISBN 978-0-9935591-3-6
Typeset in Minion Pro

Published in Great Britain by Rainbow Publications UK

About the Author

Alan was born in the city of Norwich in the county of Norfolk, England in November 1949. When Alan was still a teenager he started painting whilst attending art classes in Norwich. In his mid-teens he had two paintings accepted for a National Art Exhibition held in London and other major UK cities. Alan spent most of his working life as a professional Health and Safety Advisor and rarely picked up a paint brush until Alan, his wife Susie and daughter Ginny (his other daughter Mandy is married and lives with her husband Adrian in Sheffield) moved out of the city of Norwich into the countryside in 1993. They moved to a little village called East Lexham in the heart of Norfolk. The village was very peaceful and pretty. This helped inspire Alan to take up watercolour painting once again. In 2004 they moved to another small West Norfolk village near Downham Market where they still live today. In 2008 Alan had to retire due to ill health (bad knees) and whilst he still painted regularly he began to spend more and more time gardening. In 2013 his wife Susie suggested that he kept a gardening diary to record his adventures in the garden and capture the changing seasons, animals, birds and the successes and failures of being a gardener he encountered. By the following year Susie suggested that he should write a book from his diary and include illustrations of both the garden and his artwork. In 2014 Alan's first book was published by Creative Gateway called **"Retiring to the Garden – Year One".** This proved such a success that Alan decided to follow this up with his second book called **"Retiring into a Rainbow"** featuring his watercolour paintings. He then in 2015 published **"Retiring to Our Garden – Year Two"** published this time by Rainbow Publications UK. He then re-issued his first two books this time in a **"Second Edition"**. Also published by Rainbow Publications UK. In 2016 he published: **"Skiathos a Greek Island Paradise", "Norfolk the County of my Birth", "Art Inspired by a Rainbow", "Ibiza Island of Dreams", "Majorca Island in the Sun", "Flip-flops and Shades on Thassos", "Mardle and a Troshin' in Norfolk", "England the Country of my Birth", "Mousehole the Cornish Jewel", "Sunshine and Shades on Kefalonia", and finally "Shades and Flip-flops on Zakynthos"** Also published by Rainbow Publications UK. He has recently started on the following new books which will be entitled: **"Crete and the Island of Santorini", "Cyprus the Pyramids and the Holy Land", "Corfu and Mainland Greece", "Trips into my Mind's Eye", "Flip-flops and Shades on many Greek Islands" and finally "Greece Land of Gods and Men".** In 2020 he produced a 3rd edition of **Shades and Flip-flops on Zakynthos** also published by Rainbow Publications UK.

Alan…

I hope you will enjoy our trip to the paradise Greek Island of Zakynthos together…

Books by Alan R. Massen

Retiring to the Garden Year 1 - Paperback
Retiring into a Rainbow - Paperback and Hardback
Retiring into a Rainbow - 1st Edition - My Favourite Artwork 2020 - 1st Edition
Retiring to our Garden Year one - 1st & 2nd Editions
Retiring to our Garden Year two - 1st & 2nd & 3rd Editions
Retiring into a Rainbow - 1st & 2nd Editions
Skiathos a Greek Island Paradise - 1st & 2nd & 3rd Editions
Norfolk the County of my Birth - 1st & 2nd & 3rd Editions
Art Inspired by a Rainbow - 1st & 2nd & 3rd & 4th Editions
Ibiza Island of Dreams - 1st & 2nd Editions
Majorca Island in the Sun - 1st & 2nd Editions
Flip-Flops and Shades on Thassos - 1st & 2nd & 3rd Editions
Mardle and a Troshin' in Norfolk - 1st & 2nd Editions
England the Country of my Birth - 1st & 2nd Editions
Mousehole the Cornish Jewel - 1st & 2nd & 3rd Editions
Sunshades & Flip-Flops on Kefalonia - 1st & 2nd & 3rd Editions
Shades & Flip-Flops on Zakynthos - 1st & 2nd & 3rd Editions
Trips into my Minds Eye - 1st & 2nd & 3rd & 4th Editions
Corfu and Mainland Greece - 1st & 2nd & 3rd Editions
Crete and the Island of Santorini - 1st & 2nd & 3rd Editions
Cyprus - Pyramids - Holy Land - 1st & 2nd & 3rd Editions
Greek Islands in the Sun - 1st & 2nd & 3rd Editions
Being Greek - 1st & 2nd & 3rd Editions

E-books and Booklets:

Retiring to the Garden Yr 1 - Retiring into a Rainbow - My Art 1997 - 2018 - Skiathos a Greek Paradise Island
My Norfolk - My Greece - My England - My Team - My Skiathos - My Art - My Album of Visual Art
My Village - Greece Land of Gods and Men - Norfolk Wildlife - Civilisation (Empires of the Past)
Boudica Queen of the Iceni - Roman Britain

Susie and Alan…

Copyright © 2020 - Alan R. Massen
Published in Great Britain by Rainbow Publications UK.

Books by the same Author

by Norfolk watercolour artist - Alan R. Massen.
Published 1st Edition by Creative Gateway and 2nd Edition by Rainbow Publications UK

Books by the same Author

by Norfolk watercolour artist - Alan R. Massen.
Published in Great Britain by Rainbow Publications UK

Books by the same Author

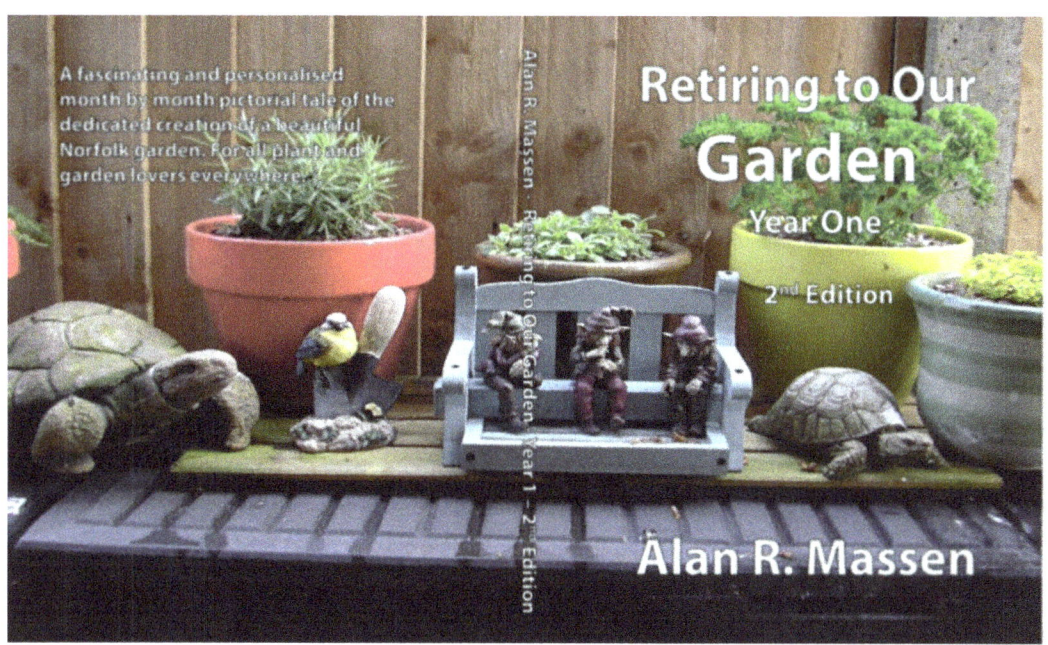

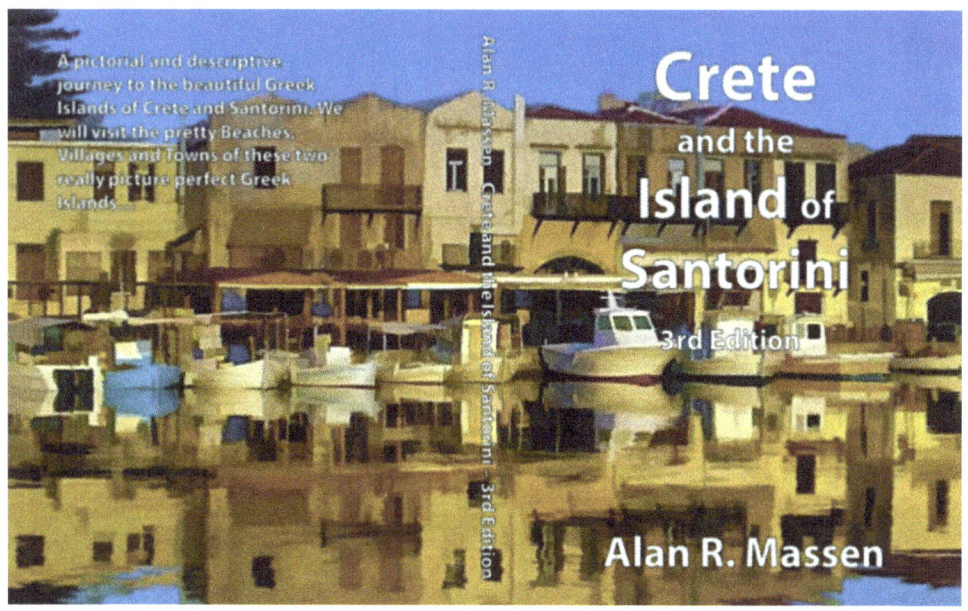

by Norfolk Watercolour Artist - Alan R. Massen
Published in Great Britain by Rainbow Publications UK

Books by the same Author

by Norfolk Watercolour Artist - Alan R. Massen
Published in Great Britain by Rainbow Publications UK

Books by the same Author

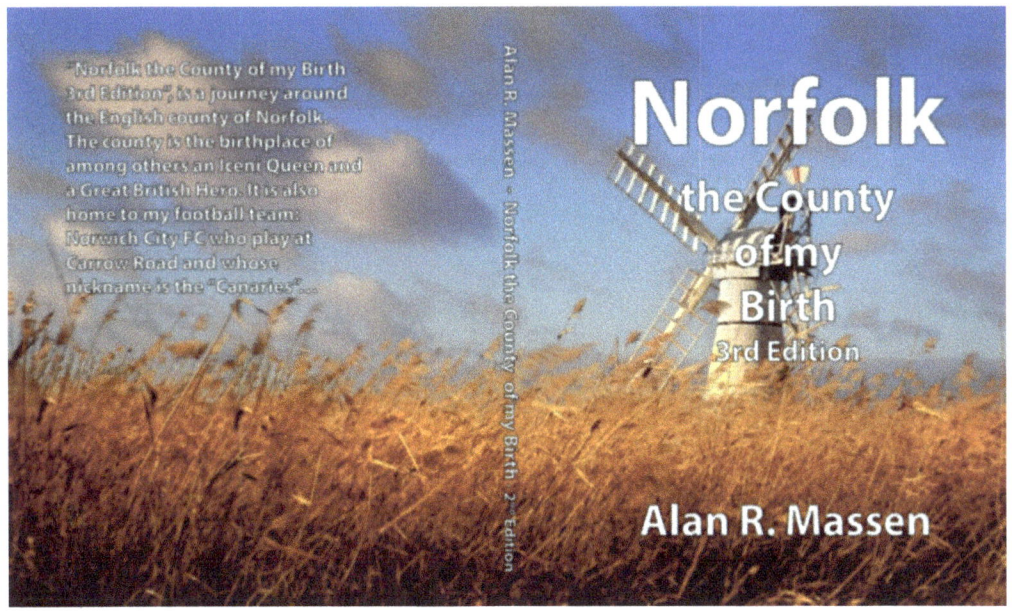

by Norfolk Watercolour Artist - Alan R. Massen
Published in Great Britain by Rainbow Publications UK

Books by the same Author

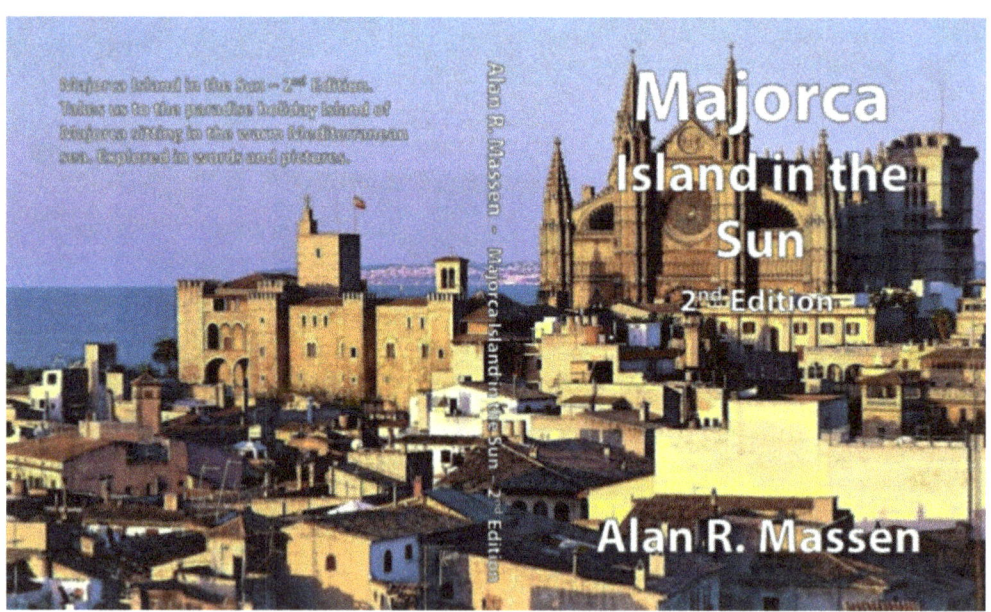

by Norfolk Watercolour Artist - Alan R. Massen
Published in Great Britain by Rainbow Publications UK

Books by the same Author

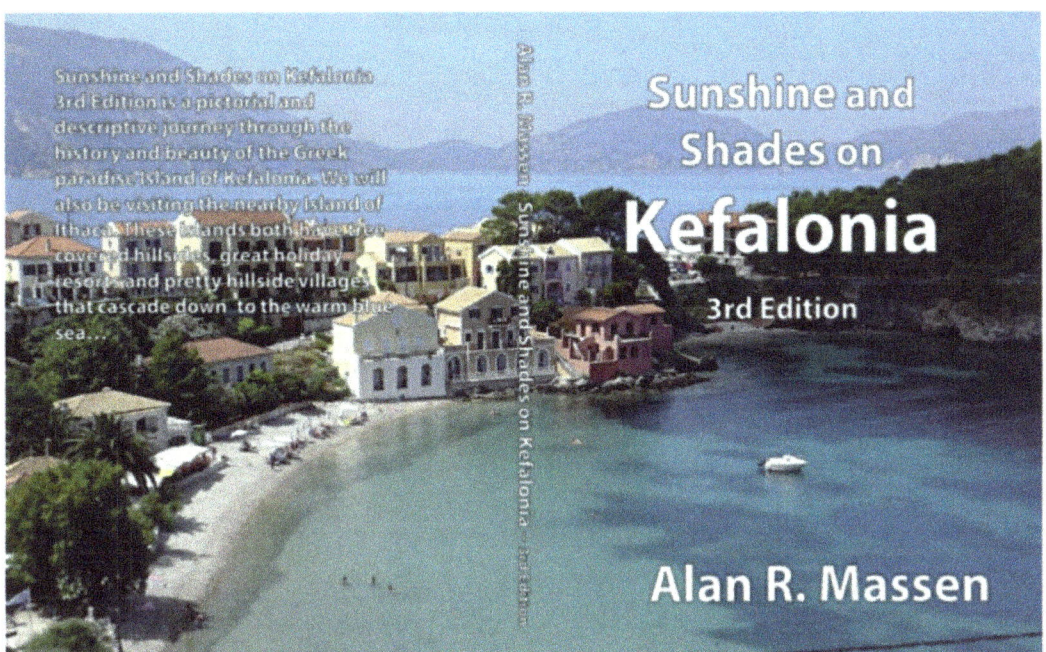

by Norfolk Watercolour Artist - Alan R. Massen
Published in Great Britain by Rainbow Publications UK

Books by the same Author

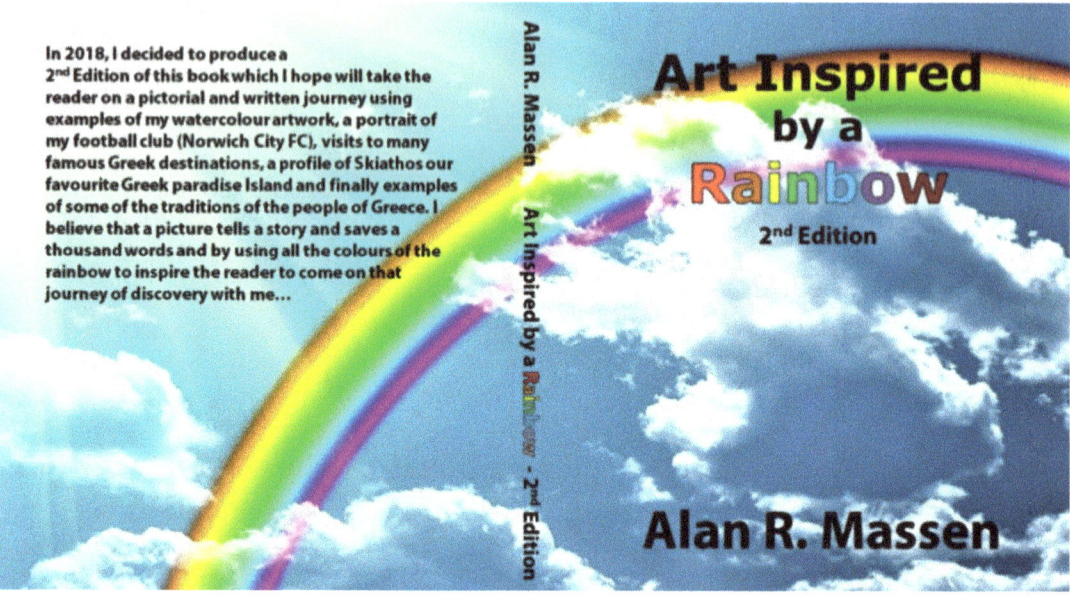

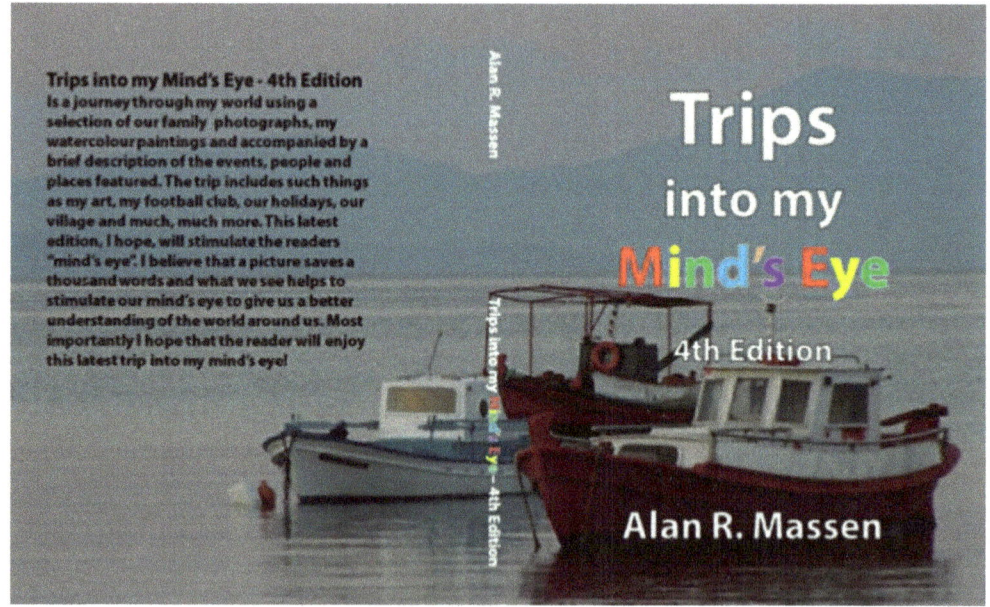

by Norfolk Watercolour Artist - Alan R. Massen
Published in Great Britain by Rainbow Publications UK

Books by the same Author

by Norfolk Watercolour Artist - Alan R. Massen
Published in Great Britain by Rainbow Publications UK

Books by the same Author

by Norfolk Watercolour Artist - Alan R. Massen
Published in Great Britain by Rainbow Publications UK

Dedication

Welcome to my book called **"Shades and Flip-flops on Zakynthos".** I would like to dedicate this book to all those people worldwide who have lost loved ones during the recent terrible Coronavirus pandemic of 2020. All those who have left us will always be remembered and live on in our hearts and minds as we remember all of the love, support and smiles that they shared with us during their lifetimes. I would also like to thank the wonderful, dedicated and brave doctors, nurses and all of the other essential workers who put their own lives at risk to help others during this tragedy. Their bravery has been an inspiration to us all during this awful time and we thank each and to every one of them. **THANK YOU**…

I would also like to dedicate this book to my wife Susie and our friends Karl, Anna, Alistair, Issy, Andrew and Lynn and all of the Zakynthians we met who all helped make our holidays to their wonderful island so enjoyable.

Times they are a Changing

It is sad to have to mention, before we start our journey together that as a UK citizen Susie and I have enjoyed being part of the fellowship of the EU for many years however, on June 23rd 2016 my countrymen and women sadly voted to leave the EU.

Now that we have reached and passed the dreaded date of the 31st January 2020 and the UK plan to finally exit the EU by the end of this year it is too early to say what impact this will have on our future foreign holiday plans to Greece and/or elsewhere. It will however, undoubtedly change many things. So if, like us, you live in the UK, be mindful that things may not now be as they were when I wrote this book.

So now that I have shared our sad news with you it is time to cheer ourselves up and visit the warm paradise Greek Island of Zakynthos in words and images.

Alan and Susie

You know what they say "a picture saves a thousand words". So if you are ready lets go…

Contents

Arriving on Zakynthos

Introduction	1
The History of Zakynthos	15
The Geography of Zakynthos	32
Information about Zakynthos	41
Out and About on Zakynthos	73
Zakynthos Town	97
Beaches-Resorts-Villages of Zakynthos	108
Our Holiday to Zakynthos	175
Zakynthos in Colour	184
Acknowledgement	202

Copyright © 2020 Alan R. Massen

Introduction

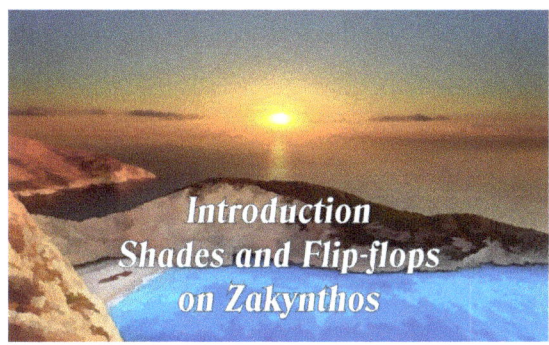

Shades and Flip-flops on Zakynthos is a pictorial and descriptive journey through the history, geography and beauty of the Greek Paradise Island of Zakynthos which is set in the blue azure Mediterranean Sea. We will visit the many great beaches, towns and villages on this really lovely holiday Island. In this book you will see numerous examples of my watercolour paintings, photographs and artwork. So if you are ready to begin we will start our journey of discovery to the island of Zakynthos…

Introduction

The Island of Zakynthos or Zante as it is sometime known, is a Greek Island located in the Ionian Sea. Zakynthos is the third largest of the Ionian Islands and it covers an area of 410 km² (158 square miles). The coastline of the Island is roughly 123 km (76 miles) in length. The Island of Zakynthos is a very popular tourist destination. It has an international airport which is served by many charter flights from all over northern Europe. The Island of Zakynthos is located 300 km west of the capital of Greece Athens and 9.5 marine miles from the mainland coast from where a regular ferry service comes and goes to and from the Island of Zakynthos…

Introduction

So now that we know something about the Island of Zakynthos and before we venture further into the pages of this book, I thought, that I ought to introduce myself for those of you that have not been on one of my many other journeys to visit other Greek Islands and far away places with me. Hello my name is Alan and I am married to Susie, we live in Norfolk, England and together, over the last twenty years, we have been fortunate enough to have had numerous summer holidays abroad. In this time our holiday destination of choice has usually been to go to one of the many fabulous Greek Islands. We have, for example, over the years, holidayed on the Islands of Corfu, Ithaca, Crete, Santorini, Thassos, Kefalonia, Skiathos and Zakynthos to name but a few. We have also visited many of the major archaeological sites on the mainland of Greece as well as spending several days wandering around the important ancient sites in the capital of Greece, Athens itself…

Introduction

Times they are a changing

It is sad to have to mention that as a UK citizen Susie and I have enjoyed being part of the fellowship of the EU for many years however, on the 31.01.2020 my countrymen and women having voted by a small majority to come out of the EU the UK left the EU. It is too early to say what impact this will have on our future foreign holiday plans to Greece or elsewhere. So if, like us, you live in the UK, be mindful that things may not now be as they were before or as they may be noted throughout this book. So now that I have introduced myself and shared our sad news with you it is time to cheer us all up and visit, in words and illustrations the warm paradise Greek Island of Zakynthos. I am pleased to say that this book contains a large selection of images. This is because, I believe, that a picture saves a thousand words! I hope you will enjoy the journey…

Introduction

The population of the Greek Island of Zakynthos is: 40,760 (2011) and covers an area of: 407.6 km² (157.4 sq. miles). People that have been to the Island of Zakynthos or Zante usually have very different opinions about the Island. Some have found their paradise, others never want to return there again. Fortunately, most people think it is a lovely Island, us included. The Island of Zakynthos enjoys a lot of summer visitors and has good tourist infrastructure. In the past we have stayed at the Venus Hotel in Kalamaki and more recently at the Louis Plagos Beach Hotel in Tragaki. Both of which were great and we enjoyed our stays at these two hotels very much. I believe that to get the most out of your holiday on the Island it largely depends on where you decide to stay on the Island. So deciding where to base yourself that will give you what you really want from your holiday will be key. I hope this book in some small way helps you select the ideal location for your time on the Island and the places you want to visit during your holiday to Zakynthos. So in other words choose carefully and you will be rewarded by having a great holiday…

Introduction

Where to base yourself for your holiday on Zakynthos is key to having a great time. It may suit you to stay in the very busy town of Laganas for example with its many taverns, bars and clubs. However, Laganas can get very crowded, busy and loud in the peak summer months. If however, you are looking for a quieter part of the Island, better suited to families you could stay in somewhere like Argassi. Whatever you want from your holiday there is somewhere to suit everyone on the Island of Zakynthos. For those of you who are looking for the more natural and beautiful side of the Island the best time to visit Zakynthos is in the spring. At this time the Island is rich in vegetation and a bounty of lovely flowers bloom just before the arrival of the package holiday makers in the summer months. The island at this time of the year (spring) is full of beautiful flowers and is a riot of colour. Perhaps for this reason, it was named fioro of Levante (the Levante flower) in ancient times…

Introduction

The Greek Island of Zakynthos is famous for its fabulous wine from its many vineyards. This is probably the reason that during ancient times, the Island of Zakynthos, was said to have been protected by the Greek God Dionysus, (the god of wine). Dionysus is the Greek god of the grape harvest, winemaking and wine, of ritual madness, fertility, theatre and religious ecstasy in Greek mythology. Alcohol, especially wine, played an important role in Greek culture with Dionysus being an important reason for this life style. He may have been worshipped as early as c. 1500–1100 BC by the Mycenaean Greeks. Evidence of a Dionysian-type cult has also been found in ancient Minoan Crete. He is a major, popular figure in Greek mythology and religion. Dionysus was the last god to be accepted onto Mt. Olympus. He was the youngest and the only one to have a mortal mother. His festivals were the driving force behind the development of Greek theatre. The famous poet Dionysios Solomos, who was the National Poet of Greece was born on the Island of Zakynthos and is best remembered for writing the Greek National anthem. Zakynthians are very proud of their music and dance heritage and are also very fond of their tradition of Greek shadow theatre which is still preformed on the Island today. You will also find, even today, many local men have the first name of Dionysios…

Introduction

The Island of Zakynthos is well known as the Island of songs and serenade, and indeed there are many local serenades and songs heard today. These are usually sung by groups of men at restaurants and other places as well as at local festivals. The first school of music in Greece was founded on the Island of Zakynthos. Music (or *mousike*) was an integral part of life in the ancient Greek world, and the term covered not only music but also dance, lyrics, and the performance of poetry. A wide range of instruments were used to perform music which was played on all manner of occasions such as religious ceremonies, festivals, private drinking parties (*symposia*), weddings, funerals, and during athletic and military activities. Music was also an important element of Greek education and dramatic performances held in theatres such as plays, recitals, and competitions. The Island of Zakynthos also has a National Marine Park, which was established here in 1999 in order to protect the endangered sea turtle Caretta-Caretta. The species of turtle lives in Greek waters and is threatened by extinction, and this was the reason for the creation of the Marine Park, so that the turtles can lay their eggs undisturbed. In the National Marine Park today, many local and foreign volunteers work to help protect these endangered animals…

Introduction

Having introduced the Island of Zakynthos to you and before we move on we will see some pictures of this lovely Island…

Introduction

Above are some more images of this lovely Island…

Introduction

Even more images of this lovely Island…

Introduction

More images of this lovely Island…

Introduction

More images of this lovely Island…

Introduction

So after seeing some of the beautiful sights of Zakynthos and having introduced myself and the Island of Zakynthos we will, in the next chapter, learn something about the history of this lovely Greek Island…

The History of Zakynthos

There are indications that the Island of Zakynthos was inhabited from the Neolithic period, 3,000 years BC. The ancient name of the island was Yria. According to another theory it is believed that the first settlers came to the Island of Zakynthos in the 16th century from the Peloponnese (mainland Greece). According to Homer (Homer is best known as the author of the Iliad and the Odyssey - He was believed by the ancient Greeks to have been the first and the greatest of the epic poets), the first King of the Island was Zakynthos, son of the King of Troy Dardanos. He created the first citadel on the Island called the Psofida. The Zakynthian later gained independence for the Island from Ithaca. Ithaca or Ithaka is a Greek Island located in the Ionian Sea, off the northeast coast of Kefalonia and to the west of continental Greece. Ithaca has an area of 120 square kilometres and a little more than three thousand inhabitants. It is the second-smallest of seven main Ionian Islands, after Paxi. The capital, Vathy or Ithaki, has one of the world's largest natural harbours. For more than six centuries they had a democracy on the Island. It was during this period that they created the colony of Zakantha…

The History of Zakynthos

There are some famous people linked with the Island of Zakynthos one of those was Hannibal who was a general of the Carthaginian army and lived in the 2nd and 3rd century B.C. He was born into a Carthaginian military family and was made to swear hostility toward Rome. The Second Punic War, also referred to as The Hannibalic War and the War against Hannibal, lasted from 218 to 201 BC and involved combatants in the western and eastern Mediterranean. This was the second major war between Carthage and the Roman Republic. They are called the "Punic Wars" because Rome's name for Carthaginians was Poeni, derived from Poenici, a reference to the founding of Carthage by Phoenician settlers. During the Second Punic War, Hannibal swept across all of southern Europe and also over the Alps, consistently defeating the Roman army, but never taking the city itself. Rome counterattacked and he was forced to return to Carthage where later he was defeated. He worked for a time as a statesman before he was forced into exile by Rome. To avoid capture by the Romans, he eventually took his own life. During his lifetime this famous general Hannibal also invaded Zakantha (Zakynthos) in 219 BC which saw the beginning of the second Punic war with the Romans. The Island was part of the Athenian alliance, and after the defeat of the alliance the Island was then ruled by the Spartans from mainland Greece. Sparta was a prominent city-state in ancient Greece. In antiquity the city-state was known as Lacedaemon, while the name Sparta referred to its main settlement on the banks of the Eurotas River in Laconia, in south-eastern Peloponnese. Around 650 BC, it rose to become the dominant military land-power in ancient Greece…

The History of Zakynthos

In the Classical era, when Philip II of Macedonia and his son Alexander the Great expanded the Macedonian border, Zakynthos was incorporated into their empire. Philip II of Macedon was the king of the Ancient Greek kingdom of Macedon from 359 BC until his assassination in 336 BC. He was a member of the Argead dynasty, the third son of King Amyntas III, and father of Alexander the Great and Philip III. Alexander III of Macedon, commonly known as Alexander the Great, was a King of the Ancient Greek kingdom of Macedon and a member of the Argead dynasty. Born in Pella in 356 BC, Alexander succeeded his father, Philip II, to the throne at the age of twenty. He spent most of his ruling years on an unprecedented military campaign through Asia and northeast Africa, and by the age of thirty he had created one of the largest empires of the ancient world, stretching from Greece to Egypt into Iran and northwest south Asia. He was undefeated in battle and is widely considered one of history's most successful military commanders. The Romans invaded the Island of Zakynthos in the 2nd century BC. The Roman Empire was characterised by government headed by emperors and large territorial holdings around the Mediterranean Sea in Europe like the Island of Zakynthos, Africa and Asia. The city of Rome was the largest city in the world c. 100 BC – c. 400 AD, with Constantinople becoming the largest around 500 AD, and the Empire's populace grew to an estimated 50 to 90 million inhabitants…

The History of Zakynthos

On the Island of Zakynthos during the Byzantine rule the Island of Zakynthos never fell under Turkish rule, but was under the Venetians instead. The Byzantine Empire, sometimes referred to as the Eastern Roman Empire, was the continuation of the Roman Empire in the East during Late Antiquity and the Middle Ages era, when its capital city was Constantinople. The most prominent leaders at that time belonged to the Orsini family, and the Venetian rule was to last for more than 300 years. The Venetians divided the residents of the Island into three categories, the aristocrats, the only ones who had political rights, the middle class and the ordinary people (popolo). It was because of their harsh treatment of the common people and the imposition of high taxes that the people tried to revolt in 1630 AD. This revolt was defeated and was followed by even more strict oppression of the people of Zakynthos…

The History of Zakynthos

In the 18th century the army of Napoleon conquered the Island of Zakynthos in 1797 AD. He was accepted by the islanders as a liberator. Napoléon Bonaparte was a French military and political leader who rose to prominence during the French Revolution and led several successful campaigns during the Revolutionary Wars. As Napoleon I, he was Emperor of the French from 1804 AD until 1814 AD, and again in 1815 AD. The people of the Island of Zakynthos thus gained more freedom than they had ever had before. Two year later came two years of Turkish-Russian administration. In 1800 AD the peace treaty between Russia and Turkey created the first independent state of Greece in the Ionian Islands. The independence of the Island was only for seven short years and in 1807 AD the French occupied Zakynthos and later came the British from 1809 AD until 1864 AD when finally the Island of Zakynthos was united with the rest of Greece…

The History of Zakynthos

Summary

It is believed that the Island of Zakynthos was inhabited from the Neolithic Age, as some digs at archaeological excavations on the Island has proven, then it is true that people have lived on the Island of Zakynthos from a very early period. The ancient Greek poet Homer mentioned the Island in the Iliad and the Odyssey. It is thought that the first inhabitants of the Island of Zakynthos was the son of King Dardanos of Troy called Zakynthos and his men. In mythology the Island was then conquered by King Arkesios of Kefalonia and then by King Odysseus of Ithaca. Later on, a treaty was signed that made Zakynthos an independent democracy, the first to be established in Greece, which lasted for more than 650 years. Zakynthos made an alliance with Athens during the First Peloponnesian War, sometime between 459 BC and 446 BC. The importance of this alliance for Athens was that it provided them with a source of tar. Tar is a more effective protector of ships planking than pitch. The Athenian fleet needed protection from rot and decay so this new source of tar was very valuable to them. The tar was dredged up from the bottom of a lake (now known as Lake Keri) using leafy myrtle branches tied to the ends of poles. It was then collected in pots that could be carried to the beach and be swabbed directly onto the ships hulls. Alternatively, the tar , in pots, could be shipped to the Athenian naval boat yard at Piraeus for storage…

The History of Zakynthos

On the Island of Zakynthos during the Middle-Ages, the Island was part of the Byzantine Empire. After 1185 AD it became part of the County of Cephalonia and Zakynthos. This lasted until the Ottomans took over in 1479 AD. The Turkish rule lasted only until 22nd April 1484 AD. It was then exchanged and become part of the Venetian Republic. The Island of Zakynthos remained an overseas colony of the Venetian Republic until its very end in 1797 AD. This way Venetian rule protected the Island of Zakynthos from Ottoman domination but in its place it put a feudal oligarchy. The cultural influence of Venice (and of Venetian on local dialect) was considerable. The wealthy made a habit of sending their sons to Italy to be educated. From the 16th to the 18th centuries, the Island of Zakynthos was one of the largest exporters of currants in the world together with Cephalonia (Kefalonia). The Treaty was ended after the dismantling of the Venetian Republic who then awarded the Ionian Islands to France…

The History of Zakynthos

The French expeditionary force with boats captured in Venice, took control of the Islands on the 26th June 1797 AD. A Russian-Turkish fleet captured the Island of Zakynthos on the 23rd October 1798 AD. From 1800 AD to 1807 AD, Zakynthos was under the sovereignty and protection of the Ottoman Empire and by Russia. In 1800–1801 AD, Great Britain attempted to take control of the Ionian island's from Zakynthos after a revolt, under the leadership of James Callander Campbell but these intentions stopped after the Peace of Amiens. After a second period under French control (1807–1809 AD) following the Treaty of Tilsit, it was conquered, by Great Britain on the 16th October 1809 AD, and the Island of Zakynthos was part of the British protectorate of the United States of the Ionian Islands from 1815 to 1864 AD. In 1864 AD, the Island of Zakynthos, together with all the other Ionian Islands, became a full member of the Greek state, ceded by Great Britain to stabilise the rule of the newly crowned Danish-born King of the Hellenes, George the First…

The History of Zakynthos

The Recent History of the Island of Zakynthos

On the Island of Zakynthos during the 19th and 20th centuries few acts of heroism could match that of two local men who during the Nazi (German) occupation of Greece during the Second World War defied their enemies. Mayor Karrer and Bishop Chrysostomos refused Nazi orders to turn in a full list of the members of the town's Jewish community for deportation to the death camps. This they refused to do and instead they hid the town's 275 Jews in rural villages all around the Island. By doing this every Jew of Zakynthos survived the war. In 1978, Yad Vashem, of the Holocaust Martyrs' and Heroes' Remembrance Authority in Israel, honoured Bishop Chrysostomos and Mayor Loukas Karrer with the title of "Righteous among the Nations", an honour given to non-Jews who, at personal risk, saved Jews during the Holocaust. After the war, all of the Jews of Zakynthos moved either to Israel or to Athens. The visitor will find statues of the Bishop and the Mayor to commemorate their heroism on the site of Zakynthos Town's historic Jewish synagogue which unfortunately was destroyed completely in the terrible earthquakes that hit the Island in 1953…

The History of Zakynthos

Greek Gods…

In more recent times the Island of Zakynthos suffered a series of four severe earthquakes in August 1953, resulting in the total destruction of its infrastructure, including most of the state archives. The 1953 Ionian earthquake struck the southern Ionian Islands in Greece on August 12th. By mid-August there were over 113 recorded earthquakes in the region between Kefalonia and Zakynthos, and the most destructive was the one on August 12th 1953. The third and most destructive of these quakes, registering 7.3 on the Richter scale, occurred at 09:24 UTC (11:24 am local time) on the 12th August 1953. It had its epicentre directly on the southern tip of the nearby Island of Kefalonia, also causing widespread destruction there as well. The quake was felt by people throughout most of the country, and only three buildings on the Island of Zakynthos were left standing after the disaster. Many Greek people felt that the Gods had deserted them!…

The History of Zakynthos

On the Island of Zakynthos after the enormous earthquake, the Island's roads that had been destroyed were re-instated, expanded and paved. Another major boast for the Island of Zakynthos was when its long awaited international airport was opened in the 1960's. Zakynthos International Airport "Dionysios Solomos" is the airport of Zakynthos, Greece. The airport is located close to the town of Kalamaki. Planes are not permitted to land or depart from 12 AM to 4 AM. This is due to the endangered loggerhead turtles or "caretta-caretta" which lay their eggs on the beaches at night. The Greek authorities can and have permitted planes to take off or land at night, but this is very rare. The airport opened in 1972. The airport is 4.3 km from Zakynthos Town and other seaside tourist destinations such as Lagana, Tsilivi and Kalamaki are nearby. The main approach into the airport is Runway 34, meaning aircraft have to fly over Lagana bay and make a 180-degree turn, before flying over the sunbathing tourists on the busy Kalamaki beach just before landing. The Island's population which had diminished in the past has risen again in more recent years due largely to tourism. On the Island of Zakynthos mining was once very common. In recent years a small mountain located on the west side of Zakynthos was mined during the 1990's, though it is no longer in use. Today mining continues on the Island of Zakynthos with two quarries on the mountain range on the western part of the Island…

The History of Zakynthos

Alan and Susie on holiday on the Island of Zakynthos…

In recent years tourism has continued to thrive on the Island and the Island of Zakynthos is currently one of the most popular tourist destinations in Greece. Travellers to the Island should be aware, as already mentioned, that the Ionian Islands are situated upon one of Europe's most notorious faults, capable of producing earthquakes potentially causing both widespread damage and considerable loss of life. They should therefore, be assured that all the buildings have been built on a swimming slab of concrete which are re-enforced with steel rods. On the Island of Zakynthos, you will be pleased to learn, the local government is determined to ensure visitor safety. The local population of Zakynthos in 2015 was more than 41,000. It is also a sad fact that the population of Zakynthos suffers from an exceptionally high rate of blindness of about 1.8%. That rate is about nine times the average found in other parts of Europe…

The History of Zakynthos

Before we leave the history of the Island behind we will enjoy some more images of this lovely Island…

The History of Zakynthos

More images of this lovely Island…

The History of Zakynthos

More images of this lovely Island…

The History of Zakynthos

More images of this lovely Island…

The History of Zakynthos

As we leave this chapter on the history of the Island we will, in the next chapter, look at the geography of the Island of Zakynthos…

The Geography of Zakynthos

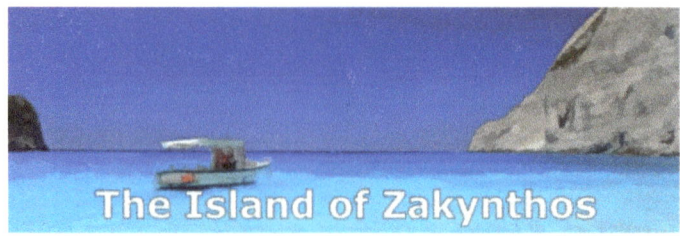

Zakynthos or Zante is a Greek Island in the Ionian Sea. It is the third largest of the Ionian Islands. Zakynthos is a separate regional unit of the Ionian Islands region, and its only municipality. It covers an area of 410 km² and its coastline is roughly 123 km in length. The name, like all similar names ending in -nthos, is pre-Mycenaean or Pelasgian in origin. In Greek mythology the Island was said to be named after Zakynthos, the son of a legendary Arcadian chief Dardanus. The Island of Zakynthos lies in the eastern part of the Ionian Sea, around 20 kilometres (12 miles) west of the Greek Peloponnese mainland. The Island of Kefalonia lies 15 kilometres (9 miles) to the north. It is the southernmost of the main group of the Ionian Island's (not counting distant Kythira). The Island of Zakynthos is about 40 kilometres (25 miles) long and up to 20 kilometres (12 miles) wide. It covers an area of 410 km² (158 square miles). Its coastline is approximately 123 km (76 miles) long and it has many beautiful beaches…

The Geography of Zakynthos

The Island of Zakynthos, according to a recent census, has a population of more than 46,000. The highest point on the Island is the mountain known as Vrachionas, at 758 m. The Island of Zakynthos is the shape of an arrowhead, with the "tip" (Cape Skinari) pointing northwest. The western half of the Island is a mountainous plateau and the southwest coast consists mostly of steep cliffs. The eastern half is a densely populated fertile plain with long sandy beaches. The peninsulas of Vassilikos on the north and Marathia on the south enclose the wide and shallow bay of Laganas on the southeast part of the Island. Laganas is the best known resort on Zakynthos due to its great nightlife reputation. It is the largest and liveliest resort on the Island and is to be found on the south coast of Zakynthos. Small hills line the resort and these gradually rise to the mountains. The resort itself is mainly flat land which hugs the large sweeping bay forming the long, popular sandy Lagana beach. Much of the accommodation in and around Lagana is surrounded by verdant scenery such as olive groves and fruit orchards. Laganas has one of the best beaches on the Island; a huge beach of about 5 km long with soft golden sand that gently shelves into the warm crystal clear waters of the Ionian Sea. This beach is part of the National Marine Park, set up to protect in particular the endangered loggerhead turtles as well as all the diverse flora and fauna found in the vicinity. The beach is used as one of the breeding beaches for the Caretta-Caretta turtles. Boat trips, for visitors, are available to see these majestic creatures swimming gracefully in the crystal clear waters off Lagana beach. …

The Geography of Zakynthos

The most famous beach on the Island of Zakynthos is known as the Shipwreck Beach, with exceptional white sand and the remains of a ship stranded on shore. Navagio Beach, or Shipwreck Beach, is an exposed cove, sometimes referred to as "Smugglers Cove". Navagio Beach was originally known as Agios Georgios. On October 2, 1980, a freightliner, the MV Panagiotis, ran aground in the waters around Zakynthos Island right on Navagio Beach after stormy weather and bad visibility. Many people falsely claim the ship was smuggling contraband cigarettes, wine and women. Although and recently, MV "PANAGIOTIS" Captain Charalambos Kompothekras - Kotsoros released the real story about what happened. The ship was actually abandoned and it still rests with its hull buried in the white sandy dunes on the beach that now holds the famous nickname Navagio Beach. If you visit the Island you just have to visit this beach and write your name on the infamous shipwrecks hull. We did!…

The Geography of Zakynthos

The soft sand of the beaches on the Island of Zakynthos create the perfect conditions for the Mediterranean sea turtle Caretta-Caretta to lay its eggs. They usually go to the beaches of Laganas and Tsilivi. Popular breeding places for the caretta-caretta are also two small islets on the southern side of Zakynthos called Pelouzo and Marathonisi. The islet of Pelouzo is on the gulf of Laganas, opposite the beach of Dafni and next to the islet called Marathonisi. Pelouzo is uninhabited and is rocky, with a small nice cave to explore. Its best feature is the beach of extremely fine sand and crystal clear water. This small islet is where the Caretta-Caretta sea turtles go to lay their eggs. The islet is protected and it is not prohibited to stay on Pelouzo after sunset. As the region is a protected area for turtles, boats are not allowed to go there. The only way to visit the islet is to swim there. It takes about two hours to swim to the islet from Dafni beach to the islet of Pelouzo but should only be atempted by strong compitent swimmers. The Island of Marathonisi (or Island of Marathias). The Island has two reefs, called Pontikonisia, that in ancient times were linked to the cape of Marathias. The Island has roughly a one mile perimeter. The Island has no inhabitants. The Island has rich vegetation, olive trees, green oaks and pine trees. On the islets long golden sandy beach the turtles Caretta-Caretta make their nests. The Guards of the National Marine Park are stationed there on a permanent basis in order to protect the island, the turtles and also their precious eggs from intruders. You can only visit the Island during daylight hours by renting a small boat from the beach of Keri, or with the Caiques that go there every day. The Island is virgin, therefore make sure that you carry enough water and other supplies with you if you intend to stay there for the day and please remember to leave nothing but your foot prints behind when you leave…

The Geography of Zakynthos

Now that we have explored the wonderful geography of Zakynthos we will now, before we move on, we will enjoy seeing some of the wildlife and other images seen on this lovely Island…

The Geography of Zakynthos

Above is a cat leaping over a bridge on the seashore of this lovely Island…

The Geography of Zakynthos

Above are more images of this lovely Island…

The Geography of Zakynthos

More images of this lovely Island…

The Geography of Zakynthos

Having explored the geography and seen some more images of the Island we will, in the next chapter, glean some useful information about the Island of Zakynthos…

Information about Zakynthos

The capital of the Island of Zakynthos, which has the same name as the prefecture, is the Town of Zakynthos. It lies on the eastern part of the northern coast. Apart from the official name, it is also called Chora (i.e. the Town, a common denomination in Greece when the name of the island itself is the same as the name of the principal town). The port of Zakynthos has a ferry connecting it to the port of Kyllini on the Greek mainland. Kyllini is the gateway to mainland Greece for people staying/living on Zakynthos and Kefalonia, however it is a destination in its own right, with plenty to do for both tourists and locals. The once small port has been developed in recent years to become a large and industrious link between the Ionian Islands and mainland Greece. Kyllini is blessed with 11km of white sandy beaches, and traditionally has surrounding hills of olive trees. The clear waters of the Ionian Sea is perfect for sun bathing and swimming…

Information about Zakynthos

The Climate and Produce of Zakynthos

The Island of Zakynthos (Zante) has a mild, Mediterranean climate and the plentiful winter rainfall endow the Island with dense green vegetation. On the Island of Zakynthos the principal agricultural products are olive oil, currants, grapes and citrus fruit. Olive oil is a fat obtained from the olive, a traditional tree crop of the Mediterranean Basin. The oil is produced by pressing whole olives and is commonly used in cooking, cosmetics, pharmaceuticals, and soaps, and as a fuel for traditional oil lamps. Olive oil is used throughout the world and is often associated with Mediterranean cuisine and diet. The famous Zante currant is a small sweet seedless grape which is native to the island. A grape is a fruiting berry of the deciduous woody vines of the botanical genus Vitis. Grapes can be eaten raw or they can be used for making wine, jam, juice, jelly, grape seed extract, raisins, vinegar, and grape seed oil. Grapes are a non-climacteric type of fruit, generally occurring in clusters. Citrus fruit come from a tree of a genus that includes citron, lemon, lime, orange, and grapefruit. Citrus trees are cultivated in warm countries for their fruit. The Island of Zakynthos grows all these types of produce in abundance…

Information about Zakynthos

When to come to Zakynthos

May is the beginning of the summer season on the Island and has reasonably hot days but fresh evenings. The Island of Zakynthos (Zante) is still relatively empty with few tourists about and this is the ideal time to find those empty and relaxing beaches. The sea is still quite cool but is mostly flat as there are no strong winds blowing at this time of year. The Island of Zakynthos is also very colourful and beautiful in May and you will see many varieties of native flowers in full bloom. May is a really great time to visit the Island of Zakynthos…

Information about Zakynthos

When to come to Zakynthos

In June the temperature starts to get very warm and the sandy beaches and clear blue sea become the perfect place to be all day long. In June the temperature of the sea also begins to rise and is just perfect for swimming and relaxing in and therefore the beaches begin to become more crowded with tourists. June is also the best month to enjoy a comfortable night's sleep before the high temperatures of July and August…

Information about Zakynthos

When to come to Zakynthos

The temperature in the month of July on the Island is very warm, but there is a welcoming fresh wind that blows in from the sea every afternoon. The month of July is also the month when tourism really kicks off and people from all over Europe come to Zakynthos Island to enjoy their summer holidays. In July, in order to sleep well at night, it would be a good idea to have air conditioning available in your room or apartment if possible…

Information about Zakynthos

When to come to Zakynthos

In August the Island of Zakynthos enjoys the same hot weather as it has in July but with much more humidity. In August on the Island of Zakynthos it is full of tourists, especially from Italy, who fill the beaches by day and the night clubs by night. This is the ideal month for those who love night life, excitement, sunny days, warm nights and crowds of people…

Information about Zakynthos

When to come to Zakynthos

In September the temperature begins to cool and becomes nice and comfortable by night. Many find that the beaches are less crowded at this time of the year and are now perfect in the midday sun. In September there are a few rainy days but these quickly change back to clear blue sky and hot sunshine. If you prefer a more peaceful holiday then September is the perfect month for you without mass tourism disturbing your peace and tranquility…

Information about Zakynthos

Documents to take with you to Zakynthos

If you are an E. U. citizens no special papers are needed to visit Greece, all the other citizens of the world need is their passports and for more info they can contact their embassies or consulates in Greece. As a UK citizen Susie and I have enjoyed being part of the fellowship of the EU for many years however, my countrymen and women voted to come out of the EU. We left on the 31st January 2020, and although it is too early to say what impact this will have on UK citizens on future foreign holidays to Greece or elsewhere but it is likely to mean changes and more costs for future holidays abroad. So if, like us, you live in the UK, be mindful that sadly things may not now be as easy as they were before…

Information about Zakynthos

The import of Animals onto the Island

If you want to bring any animals to the Island of Zakynthos they will need a health certificate to prove that the animal has had an antirabic prophylaxis protection jab against rabies. The validity of the certificate has to be more than 12 months for dogs, more than 6 months for cats and it has to be dated for at least 6 days before the arrival of the animal on the Island of Zakynthos…

Information about Zakynthos

Health issues

When you visit the Island it is nice to know that in Zakynthos town there is a hospital where you can ask for help if you need it. There are a few private clinics and doctors who speak English in the city and you will find, in almost every village, there is a pharmacy.

Clothing - What to wear

On the Island of Zakynthos you can wear what you like and it is only in churches and monasteries that more formal clothes are required (trousers or long skirts and t-shirts with sleeves). Some churches supply shawls to the visitor who arrive inappropriately dressed to use during their visit…

Information about Zakynthos

Time on Zakynthos

In the summertime, Greece is two hours ahead of the time in the UK (Greenwich meridian time) like elsewhere in Europe. Also in Greece, in the summer season (March – September) you will find that there is something very curious about time. In Greece it is conceived in a very particular way. Here time is not running, there is no such concept of "being on time or being late" and a watch is just something to wear. The Greeks themselves are aware of the need for them to take it easy (but not in serving the tourist!) up to the point that G.M.T. is not considered as the Greenwich Meridian Time, but as the Greek Maybe Time! So remember you are on holiday take your time and relax things will get done in the fullness of time or should I say in Greek time…

Information about Zakynthos

Electricity supply

On the Island of Zakynthos, like the rest of Greece the electrical socket outlets are double pronged and not triple pronged as they are in the UK. Therefore I suggest that you always travel to the Island of Zakynthos with an adaptor so you can still use any UK mains electrical equipment that you may have taken with you.

Roads on the Island

The Island has an efficient road network, with main roads, secondary and non-asphalted ones leading to most places. The roads however, on Zakynthos Island may not always be in good condition (much like ours at home). So be careful when driving around the Island and don't forget to wear your seat (safety) belt! Drive responsibly at all times and have a great, happy, healthy and safe holiday…

Information about Zakynthos

Phoning home by public telephone

On the Island of Zakynthos there are many public telephone boxes from which it is possible to make telephone calls with pre-paid telephone cards that you can buy in every local shop. It is possible to make national and international telephone calls also from the OTE's office (Greek Organization of Telecommunications) open from Monday to Friday from 8:00 to 14:00. Your accommodation provider will almost certainly provide a telephone, for your use, in your room (charges however, may be rather expensive). These days most people have their own mobile phone with them on holiday and use those however, check with your service provider to make sure that you are on the cheapest tariff available whilst abroad. Do not forget to take your mobile phone charger and adaptor with you. If you travel with a tour company they will probably give you an Island contact number to call their representatives on if you have any problems or want some advice. But remember you are on holiday too and others may not appreciate you sitting relaxing on the beach or in a bar whilst shouting into your mobile phone like so many do back in the UK…

Information about Zakynthos

Boat off Zakynthos

Ginny and Alan in Zakynthos Town…

Money on Zakynthos

Being a member of the European Union, the currency in Greece is the Euro. Most credit and debit cards can be used anywhere on the Island of Zakynthos to pay for accommodation, restaurants, rentals etc. Also you may have travellers cheque(s) that can be changed in every bank or exchange office. So remember to get yourself a few Euros to use on your outward journey and decide how you are going to pay for what you want whilst you are on the Island. So remember to pack along with your cloths your passport, tickets, luggage and any cash, cards or cheque(s) you may need during your holiday. When you are on the Island remember that tips in restaurants are not obligatory, it's up to you but good manners and politeness are free and should be generously given by you to others at all times. A please and a thank you goes a long way…

Information about Zakynthos

Famous Zakynthians

Amongst the most famous Zakynthians is the 19th-century poet Dionysios Solomos (1798–1857), poet and writer of the Greek national anthem, whose statue adorns the main town square. The Italian poet Ugo Foscolo was also born on the Island of Zakynthos. Other notable people are: Dionysios of Zakynthos (c. 16th century) a Saint of the Orthodox Church – Nikolaos Koutouzis (1741–1813) an artist – Andreas Kalvos (1789–1869) a poet and Kostas Dikefalos (born 1956) a sculptor…

Information about Zakynthos

Culture on Zakynthos

The Island of Zakynthos has a long musical tradition. The Greek love the playing of music and it was the precursor of opera in Greece. On the Island it provided a tangible link between nobles and the rest of the people. In 1815 AD, on Zakynthos, saw the establishment of the first ever Music School in the whole of Greece. During the first modern day Olympic Games in Athens in 1896 AD, the Music Band of Zakynthos had the honour of taking part in the opening ceremony. On the Island of Zakynthos the Zante Jazz Festival is held every year…

Information about Zakynthos

Susie and Alan on Zakynthos

Museums of Zakynthos

On the Island of Zakynthos there are two museums located in Zakynthos town. They are the Byzantine Museum of Zakynthos and the Museum of Solomos and Eminent People of Zakynthos, hosting the mausoleum of Dionysios Solomos and Andreas Kalvos, as well as works by many other eminent Zakynthians…

Information about Zakynthos

Transport Links to and around Zakynthos

The Island of Zakynthos is covered by a network of asphalt roads, particularly the flat eastern part of the Island. Main routes link the town of Zakynthos with Volimes on north, Keri on the south, and the peninsula of Vassiliki on the west. The road between Volimes and Lithakia is the spine of the western half of the Island. The Island has one airport, Zakynthos International Airport, "Dionysios Solomos" which connects flights from other Greek airports and numerous other tourist charter airports. The airport is located near Laganas. The Island of Zakynthos has two important ports: the main port, located in Zakynthos town, and another in the village of Agios Nikolaos. From the main port there is a regular ferry connection to the port of Kyllini, which is the usual route for arrivals to the island by sea from the mainland of Greece. From the port of Agios Nikolaos there is a regular ferry connection to the nearby holiday Island of Kefalonia (port of Pesada)…

Information about Zakynthos

Getting to Zakynthos

By air: Zakynthos' international airport 'Dionysios Solomos' serves both national and international flights all of the year round. It is located 4 km from the town centre and only 2 km from Laganas. Between May and October there are direct charter flights from various European countries including the UK, Ireland, Italy, Austria, Germany, France and Holland among many other's. If you are flying from outside the European Union you would need to fly into Zakynthos via Athens. From November through to April there are no charter flights, therefore one has to travel to Athens and take a connecting flight to the Island of Zakynthos. Daily domestic flights between Athens and the Island of Zakynthos operate throughout the year. Other connections from the Island of Zakynthos include from Kerkyra, Kefalonia and Thessaloniki…

Information about Zakynthos

Getting to Zakynthos

By ferry: People can catch a ferry from Kyllini, on the Peloponnisos side of mainland Greece. There are regular departures during the summer months. If you are travelling from Europe you can catch a ferry to Patra from Venice, Ancona, Bari or Brindizi and then, from there, another onto the Island of Zakynthos.

By car: People driving to the Island from mainland Greece drive to Kyllini and then catch a ferry as above. Driving to the Island of Zakynthos from Europe is feasible but can take up to five days.

By coach: People can travel by coach and coaches depart daily from both Athens and Patra on the mainland of Greece. From Athens International airport (Eleftherios Venizelos) take the E 93 bus service which takes you directly to Kiffisos KTEL station. From there you can catch a coach to the Island of Zakynthos (journey time up to 5 hours)…

Information about Zakynthos

Getting around the Island of Zakynthos

By Car: On the Island hiring a car is probably the best way to get around the Island and reach some of the more remote spots and see the unique views either when visiting the numerous mountain villages or by the sea. It is often cheaper to book your hire car online or as part of your holiday package before setting off on your holiday. The road system on the Island of Zakynthos is often in poor condition and tarmac can get very slippery in the summer heat (just like back home). Also be aware of the many low visibility bends, potholes and irresponsible drivers (unfortunately just like back at home) that you will encounter along the way. Ensure that you have a good road map with you and remember to keep to the speed limits at all times (not like drivers do in the UK!). Ensure you always have enough petrol as there are not too many petrol stations in the small villages, however, there are plenty on the main busy roads from and to the bigger villages, resorts and town. So if you decide to hire a car and drive around the Island you will find much to be enjoyed and all with fantastic scenery…

Information about Zakynthos

Getting around the Island of Zakynthos

By Bus: There is a local bus system (honest) but it is not the most reliable means of getting around the Island. In addition it is worth knowing that some bus services do not run at the weekends. Some of the destinations covered by the local buses that depart from Zakynthos Town are: Agalas, Agios Leon, Agios Nikolaos, Alykes, Anafonitria, Argassi, Katastari, Keri, Laganas, Volimes and Vasilikos among several others. You should however, always try to have at least one local bus journey during your stay on the Island of Zakynthos as they are usually a great experience and give the traveller a different perspective of the Island and its people. The local buses are usually well used by the locals and it may be standing room only on many trips. Remember many nationalities have a different perception of the word queuing than the British and to them it means: when the bus stops: "all rush on at once"…

Information about Zakynthos

Getting around the Island of Zakynthos

By Taxi: On the Island of Zakynthos taxis are always available everywhere you go on the Island. Your taxi fare will either be fixed (usually for tourist rides to different resorts) or, if you board a meter taxi, ensure the driver switches the day-time meter on when you board (night fares are more or less double the normal charge). People, often find, that by using taxis for their journeys that it is a relatively inexpensive and a convenient way of getting around from beach to beach or into the mountains to visit the pretty villages or to go into town…

Information about Zakynthos

Getting around the Island of Zakynthos

By Boat: When you are on holiday on the Island of Zakynthos you should definitely go on an around the Island boat trip. Various tour operators offer different packages or you can hire boats privately. Be aware that restrictions apply as to where you can go in them so check with the hirer before setting sail. You need to be aware that the Islands famous tourist destination of the Marathonissi islet, the famous Navagio (shipwreck) beach, The Blue Caves and Keri Caves can only be reached by sea. Like in the UK, the sea, plays a vital part in the communication, commerce, well being and beliefs of the people of the Island of Zakynthos and is to be enjoyed to the full at every possible opportunity during your holiday…

Information about Zakynthos

Getting around the Island of Zakynthos

Travelling around the Island by Motorbikes and/or Quad-bikes: On the Island there are plenty of outlets hiring out all sorts of mopeds and bikes. These are widely used during the summer months and unfortunately not in the most safest or sensible of ways by visitors. People should try and choose alternative means of transport where possible as quality controls and safety measures are not always up to the required standards for these types of vehicles.

By Bicycle or Walking on the Island: People can hire bicycles from a number of outlets around the Island of Zakynthos. Be extra cautious when cycling on busy roads as the local roads are not designed with cyclists or walkers in mind. Other road users and potholes are a constant danger on the Islands roads (just like back at home!) There is, however, one bicycle path on the Island found between Volimes and Anafonitria. Another picturesque location for cycling or walking is the salt flats at Alykes…

Information about Zakynthos

After all of the information in this chapter it is time for us to relax for a few pages and look at some more images of the lovely Island of Zakynthos…

Information about Zakynthos

More images of the lovely Island of Zakynthos…

Information about Zakynthos

More images of the lovely Island of Zakynthos…

Information about Zakynthos

More images of good food, honey, caves and much, much more on the Island of Zakynthos…

Information about Zakynthos

More images of the lovely Island of Zakynthos…

Information about Zakynthos

More images of the lovely Island of Zakynthos…

Information about Zakynthos

After reading about the history, geography and some useful information regarding the Island we will now move on, In the next chapter we will go Out and About on the Paradise Greek Island of Zakynthos…

Out and About on Zakynthos

When you visit the Island of Zakynthos you should always try and find the time to go and visit the sandy beaches where the loggerhead turtles Caretta-Caretta lay their eggs at night. The loggerhead sea turtle, or loggerhead, is an oceanic turtle distributed throughout the world. It is a marine reptile, belonging to the family Cheloniidae. The average loggerhead measures around 90 cm long when fully grown, although larger specimens of up to 280 cm have been discovered. The adult loggerhead sea turtle weighs approximately 135 kg, with the largest specimens weighing in at more than 450 kg. The skin ranges from yellow to brown in color, and the shell is typically reddish-brown. No external differences in gender are seen until the turtle becomes an adult, the most obvious difference being the adult males have thicker tails and shorter plastrons than the females. If you are lucky, you might also catch a glimpse of the rare Monk Seal (Monachus-Monachus). The Hawaiian monk seal, Neomonachus schauinslandi, is a highly endangered species of earless seal in the family Phocidae that is endemic to the Hawaiian Islands. The Hawaiian monk seal is one of two remaining monk seal species; the other is the Mediterranean monk seal. A third species, the Caribbean monk seal, is extinct. You can also take a boat from Agios Nikolaos, to visit the famous blue caves in the north of the Island. The blue caves are among the most famous sights of the Island with the amazing beautiful colour of the water, the largest of the caves is the cyanon cave. Another popular sight to visit is the shipwreck (Navagio) on the beach of the so called Smuggler's Bay. You should also visit the white cliffs at Keri which are reminiscent of the white cliffs of Dover in Kent, England…

Out and About on Zakynthos

Many of the beaches on the Island of Zakynthos offer water sports facilities. Porto Zorro is an excellent place for snorkelling and diving from the rocks that are on the edge of the beach. At Porto Zorro you will find a lovely beach with umbrellas as well as many bars and cafes. There are also day trips available that visit the Island of Kefalonia (Cephalonia or Kefalonia, formerly also known as Kefallinia or Kephallenia, is the largest of the Ionian Islands in western Greece) and some travel agencies even offer trips that go to Ancient Olympia on the mainland. Olympia, a sanctuary of ancient Greece in Elis on the Peloponnese peninsula, is known for having been the site of the Olympic Games in classical times…

Out and About on Zakynthos

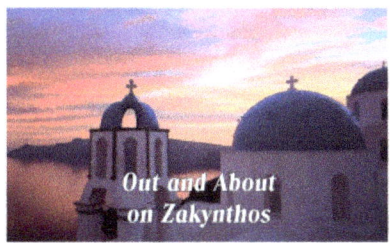

Zakynthos is an Island of big contrasts from the lovely golden beaches to high mountain scenery. Along the coast of the Island there are massive rocky formations that dive down to the shoreline of the Island. The Island of Zakynthos benefits from a Mediterranean temperate climate with mild winters and cool springs and warm/hot summers. It also has generous winter rains that helps the growth of thick lust green vegetation. This means that the Island has very good fresh water reserves. That is the reason why the Island is very "green" and in the past both Homer and the Venetian rulers used to call the Island "wooded" and "Levant flower". The very warm Mediterranean Sea water that lap the coast helps prolong the tourist season (from May till the end of October). All of this has help make the Island of Zakynthos a favourite place to visit. It is also an object of international interest especially because in the southern part of the Island the CARETTA-CARETTA turtles breed; they are a rare specimen protected by Greek legislation, in recent years, with the creation of a new marine park…

Out and About on Zakynthos

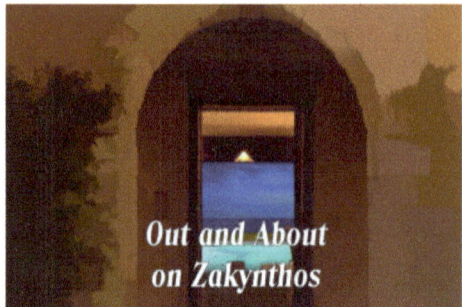

Along the rocky, western coast of Zakynthos the seals Monachus Monachus breed. The seals are also protected by the local administrative authorities. In addition to the wonderful natural landscape, Zakynthos offers the visitor the possibility of visiting numerous deserted small islands that surround it like Pelouzo and Marathonissi in the Lagana's Bay, St. John in front of Porto Vromi and the Strofades. The latter are two small islands 27 nautical miles south from the Island of Zakynthos. These Island, because of their natural beauty, are part of the protected marine park…

Out and About on Zakynthos

In the last twenty years the Island of Zakynthos has undergone a programmed plan of rigorous development to offer the tourists a modern infrastructure whilst keeping its traditional charm and traditions alive. These can be seen in the traditional tavernas/restaurants along its seashore and in the inland small villages. This traditional mix of the past together with the joy of life and hospitality of its inhabitants will touch you from the very first day that you set foot on the wonderful and welcoming Island of Zakynthos…

Out and About on Zakynthos

The Island of Zakynthos offers exceptional places for scuba divers. Caves around the island attract numerous divers. A wide range of marine life can be found, common amongst them are the moray eels (Moray eels or Muraenidae are a family of cosmopolitan eels. The approximately 200 species in 15 genera are almost exclusively marine, but several species are regularly seen in brackish water, and a few, for example the freshwater moray, can sometimes be found in fresh water), monk seals (Mediterranean monk seal), octopus (The octopus is a cephalopod mollusc of the order Octopoda. It has two eyes and four pairs of arms and, like other cephalopods, it is bilaterally symmetric. It has a beak, with its mouth at the center point of the arms. It has no internal or external skeleton, allowing it to squeeze through tight places. Octopuses are among the most intelligent and behaviorally diverse of all invertebrates), and of course the famous loggerhead turtles (caretta caretta)…

Out and About on Zakynthos

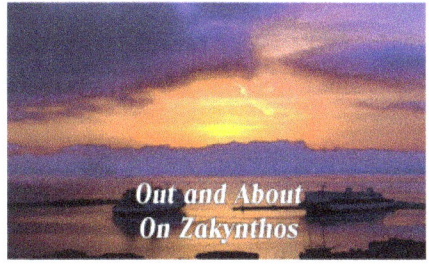

On the Island of Zakynthos, in the Bay of Laganas, is the site of the Islands very first National Marine Park and is the prime nesting area for loggerhead sea turtles (Caretta caretta) in the Mediterranean. Every year at the beginning of June, the female turtles come to the southern beaches in order to bury their eggs in the sand. The incubation period for the nest is approximately fifty-five days, after which time hatchlings emerge from the nest and make their way to the sea. The survival rate for hatchlings is very small, and it is estimated that only one in one thousand hatchlings that enter the sea lives to adulthood. Each nest contains around one hundred to one hundred and twenty eggs, each of which are around the size and shape of a ping-pong ball. Female turtles begin to make nest and lay their eggs at around twenty to thirty years of age…

Out and About on Zakynthos

The most famous landmark of the Island of Zakynthos can be found on the Navagio beach. It is a cove on the northwest shore, isolated by high cliffs and accessible only by boat. The beach and sea floor are made of white pebbles, and surrounded by turquoise waters. It is named after a shipwreck (MV Panagiotis), which sunk on the shore around 1980. Numerous "Blue Caves", are cut into cliffs around Cape Skinari, and accessible only by small boats. The sunrays reflect through the blue sea water onto the white stones of cave bottoms and walls, creating stunning visual lighting effects. Dolphins can often be seen in the waters around the Island or following boats…

Out and About on Zakynthos

The beautiful village of Keri is located in the far south of the Island of Zakynthos. It is a mountain village which has a lighthouse to the south which has a panoramic view of the southern part of the Ionian Sea. On the Island the northern and eastern shores feature numerous wide sandy beaches that attract many tourists in the summer months. Located above Zakynthos town is a small Venetian castle that offers splendid panoramic views out over the town. Located next to Bochali, Strani hill is the location where the famous Zakynthian Dionysios Solomos penned the Greek National Anthem…

Out and About on Zakynthos

The nightlife on the Island of Zakynthos is very vibrant during the summer season. Laganas gets extremely busy during the high season and it is full of music bars and night clubs, you can even find English pubs here. The resort of Argassi is a bit quieter, but it still has quite a few music bars and clubs. In Zakynthos town there are also a few bars, but it is generally quieter here and people usually spend their time wander around seeing the sights, shopping, having a drink and/or a very good meal…

Out and About on Zakynthos

The food and drink on the island of Zakynthos is of a very high standard. It ranges from local specialties such as the wonderfully named skordostoumpi, a dish with aubergines and garlic and also the meat dish sartsa. Other local foodstuff that are produced on the Island are cheeses, such as mytzithra and ladotyri. The Island of Zakynthos also produces very good wines. There is a wide variety of local and international restaurants on Zakynthos. The rule "eat where the Greeks eat" applies here as on any other Greek island. You'll find all sorts of eateries on the Island and if you just want a light meal there is always souvlaki the original Greek fast food…

Out and About on Zakynthos

Like all other holiday destinations the Island of Zakynthos has its fair share of shopping opportunities. When shopping on Zakynthos it is worth knowing that the best shopping can be found in Zakynthos town, where you can get souvenirs, cards, food, bread, cakes, clothes, pottery, icons and almost anything else the discerning shopper may require. You can also stock up on local cheeses and wine as well as the local sweets such as Mandolato (sweet made of almonds) and Pastelia a sweet made from honey and sesame. Do not forget to take some back home with you…

Out and About on Zakynthos

When visiting the Island of Zakynthos you will find that it is easy to get around the Island. The Island, as we have already heard, has a good road network. There are also local buses that go to almost everywhere on the whole island, and also a multitude of taxis and rental cars and motorbikes available to speed you on your journey. From the harbour in Zakynthos town small excursion boats will take you too many of the beaches of Zakynthos. In town you can spend an enjoyable day just walking around the small narrow streets and exploring the many hidden sights, such as the market, museums and lots of small gift shops…

Out and About on Zakynthos

Susie and I spent the whole of one day and an evening exploring Zakynthos Town during our holiday on the Island. We wandered around the town and enjoyed every moment. It is a lovely capital town. We strolled in the historic St. Mark's Square and visited the Solomos and Kalvos Museum which also houses their Mausoleum. There are also displayed original artifacts of the Island's gentry along with their personal seals. Afterwards we went to the nearby Solomos Square with all its neoclassical buildings before visiting the Byzantine Museum to marvel at the old icons and frescoes that have survived from the medieval churches of the Island that did not unfortunately survive the disastrous earthquake of 1953…

Out and About on Zakynthos

On the Island of Zakynthos you will discover some really beautiful mountain villages along with those on the plains below together with lovely hamlets and resorts by the sea-side. You may be lucky enough, on your holiday, to spot signs of activity from between the sharp edged rocks, or on the white sand or even in the turquoise water of the bays as the Caretta-Caretta sea-turtle try to find refuge and to reproduce and lay its eggs. On the beaches of Lagana and Geraka the Caretta-Caretta sea-turtle will return back to every year and lumber out of the sea, at night, up the beach and dig their nest to lay their precious eggs in before returning to the sea...

Out and About on Zakynthos

On the Island of Zakynthos the mountain villages of Keri, Lithakia, Maherado and Koiliomeno are famous for their true Zakynthian hospitality and you will really enjoy sampling the local gastronomy (food) and unsurpassed local wine. In these villages you can sample such local dishes as different cheeses, cold meat cuts and the special local sweets but most of all the semi-dry wine (mastelado) of the area will stay with you for a long time after you return home. Sgantzeto, pantseta, ladotyri, chiromeri, mantolato and pasteli are some of the wine names you must try to remember when visiting these Zakynthos villages…

Out and About on Zakynthos

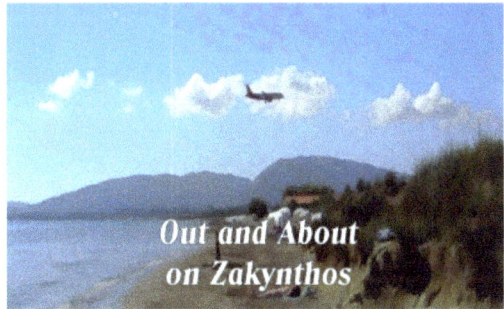

On the Island of Zakynthos, the Monasteries, are another place of interest and well worth a visit during your stay on the Island. If you take the time to learn something of the history and religious worship of the Monasteries and be lucky enough to hear the special Zakynthian way of chanting that has the power to lift your spirit to another dimension you will be glad that you took the time to visit. Whilst at the Monasteries it is also well worth taking the time to look at the lovely frescoes and old icons on display. During your visit you will experience the atmosphere, see the beauty all around the Monasteries and the see the simplicity of the way of life chosen by the Nuns and the Monks…

Out and About on Zakynthos

Above are some out and about pictures of the Island of Zakynthos…

Out and About on Zakynthos

Above are some more out and about pictures of the Island of Zakynthos…

Out and About on Zakynthos

Above are some more out and about pictures of the Island of Zakynthos…

Out and About on Zakynthos

Above are some more out and about pictures of the Island of Zakynthos…

Out and About on Zakynthos

Above are some more out and about pictures of the Island of Zakynthos…

Out and About on Zakynthos

Above are some more out and about pictures of the Island of Zakynthos…

Out and About on Zakynthos

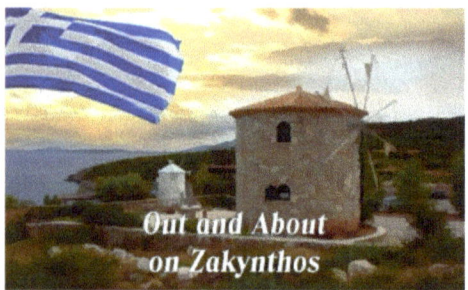

After going out and about in the villages, the blue caves, the "shipwreck" and much, much more! I suggest you explore these for yourself when you visit the Island of Zakynthos as we will now be moving on once more! In the next chapter we will be visiting the beautiful capital town of the Island of Zakynthos…

Zakynthos Town

Zakynthos Town

You will find that Solomou Square in the evening is a great place to wander around in. It is the main square in Zakynthos town and is named after the Greek National poet Dionysios Solomos. He was born on the Island of Zakynthos where he found inspiration on the Island to write his poem "Hymn to Freedom" which forms the lyrics of the Greek national anthem. A statue of Solomos dominates the square, which is a popular place on summer evenings for locals and tourists alike to take a pleasant stroll or stop for coffee in one of the nearby cafes. The square is also surrounded by many important buildings such as: the Church of Saint Nikolas on the Mole, the Byzantine Museum of Zakynthos, The Cultural Centre of Zakynthos and also the town cinema. So you can just have a coffee, eat some food or just sit and take in the sights and sounds of this vibrant town…

Zakynthos Town

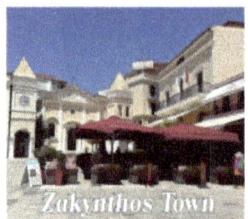

The Byzantine Museum of Zakynthos

The museum is located, as I have already mentioned, in Solomou Square, in Zakynthos town. The Byzantine Museum houses an impressive collection of hagiographies from the Byzantine era, as well as Hellenistic and Byzantine sculptures and statues, and many fine icons from the churches on the island. Zakynthos itself was home to many excellent hagiographers such as Doxaras, Koutouzis, Tzanes, Kandounis and Damaskinos and the museum exhibits examples of their work as well as paintings from the 17th and 18th Century when the Island of Zakynthos was the centre of the Ionian School of painting. The museum is well worth a visit during your stay on the Island…

Zakynthos Town

The Cultural Centre of Zakynthos Town and it's Public Library

The Cultural Centre and Public Library is located next to the church of Saint Nikolas on the Mole and is an impressive building. The Public Library is renowned as being one of the best library's in Greece and houses more than 50,000 literary works. The library also has a small art gallery, an interesting collection of dolls wearing local costumes, a photographic display of Zakynthos throughout the ages and also the historical archive of the Island of Zakynthos can be found here…

Zakynthos Town

The church of Saint Nikolaos on the Mole

The church of Saint Nikolaos was built in 1561 and is the oldest building in Solomou Square and is also the only Venetian building that survived the devastating earthquake of 1953. It is a church of great historical importance and is also an important part of Zakynthian culture as Saint Dennis, the patron saint of the Island, served for a short time at this church. Visitors to the Island should please remember the dress code, if you wish to visit the inside of the church, which is well worth seeing you will need to wear the appropriate clothing…

Zakynthos Town

The statue of Dionysios Solomos, National Poet of Greece

The statue of Dionysios Solomos is located in the square of the same name that I have already mentioned before. The statue was erected to honour Dionysios Solomou the Greek poet whose poem "Hymn to Freedom" formed the lyrics for the national anthem. The statue and the square serve to celebrate one of the Island of Zakynthos's most famous residents and the square is also the main square of Zakynthos town…

Zakynthos Town

Above are some illustrations of the beauty that is Zakynthos town…

Zakynthos Town

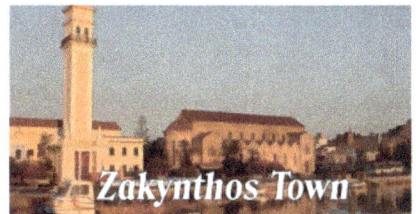

Above are some illustrations of the beauty that is Zakynthos town…

Zakynthos Town

Above are some illustrations of the beauty that is Zakynthos town…

Zakynthos Town

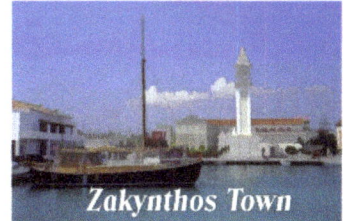 

Above are some illustrations of the beauty that is Zakynthos town…

Zakynthos Town

Above are some illustrations of the beauty that is Zakynthos town…

Zakynthos Town

Above are some final artwork of the beauty that is Zakynthos town as we say goodbye to the capital and set off in the next chapter to explore the beautiful beaches, resorts and villages that are all around the paradise Island of Zakynthos…

The Beaches, Resorts and Villages of Zakynthos

It is interesting to know that the name Zante is what the Italians called the Island in days gone by and Zakynthos is its Greek name. The Island is one of the most southerly of the Ionian chain of holiday Islands that sidle down the coast of western Greece. One of the most popular of the Greek holiday Islands, the Island of Zakynthos features prominently in many travel brochures and on line. The Island of Zakynthos is a firm favourite with travel companies offering cheap package holiday deals. The reason that the Island is so popular with holidaymaker's is that it has such lovely beaches, resorts and villages. In this chapter we will visit many of the best beaches on the Island…

The Beaches, Resorts and Villages of Zakynthos

The Island of Zakynthos has a selection of busy beaches, quiet family coves, wild and rugged cliffs, green forested hills and fertile plains in roughly equal measures. The famous beach resort of Laganas, for example, has been justifiably likened to a noisy, vibrant, busy and loud resort whilst the idyllic Port Vromi beach is a haven of peaceful tranquility. So the Island can deliver a beach, resort or village that will meet all that the visitor wants out of their holiday all you have to do is choose your holiday location carefully then sit back, relax and enjoy…

The Beaches, Resorts and Villages of Zakynthos

Two major events shaped the modern-day Island of Zakynthos. The catastrophic earthquake of 1953 which destroyed almost all of the island's elegant Venetian mansions while the construction of the airport precipitated the rise of Zakynthos's reputation for good value family fun packed beach holidays. The busiest beach resorts are north-west of the capital city of Zakynthos Town and along the huge bay of Laganas, to the south. Elsewhere, visitors can expect pretty village tavernas, quiet beach coves and lots of beautiful scenery, especially along the wild western coast of the Island…

The Beaches, Resorts and Villages of Zakynthos

On such a large Island as Zakynthos you would expect there to be a wide variety of resorts, beaches, villages and Zakynthos certainly lives up to that expectation. The longest sandy beach strips are found north-west of Zakynthos Town and around the bay of Laganas. Those who enjoy loud music and big screen TV will enjoy staying in resorts like Alykes and Laganas. Those seeking a more sedate spot will head south-east to the peninsula at Vasilikos or the resort of Keriou Limnou in the south-west of the Island of Zakynthos…

The Beaches, Resorts and Villages of Zakynthos

In general the beaches on the Island of Zakynthos are excellent for families with children. There is also the very famous shipwreck beach which you can only visit by boat. In the busy resort town of Laganas there is a 9 km sandy beach. The resorts of Argassi and Alikes can also get extremely busy in the summer months. At the Vasilikos peninsula the beaches are well suited for children and their sand castles and paddling requirements. The only thing you have to look out for when you are travelling out and about on the Island, looking for a nice beach, is to make sure that it has no signs or fences to advise visitors that the beach is off limits because the turtles are nesting there. These places must be left alone and you must therefore, move on but remember there is always another beautiful sandy beach just around the next corner on the Island of Zakynthos…

The Beaches, Resorts and Villages of Zakynthos

Venus Hotel…

On the Island of Zakynthos you will find another nice beach near Keri Lake called not surprisingly Keri beach. Just opposite this beach is the small Island of Marthonissos. There are so many beautiful places to visit on the Island I recommend that you get yourself an Island map as soon as you arrive. Another great place to visit is the village of Xirokastelo which has the beaches of Daphne and Sekania close by. Not far from Porto Zoro you will find the famous Banana beach which is very popular with young people. In Kalamaki, where we stayed at the Venus Hotel some years ago, the beach is of white sand and is fringed by dunes. On both sides of the beach front there are white cliffs. You will find that some parts of this very long beach may be fenced and signed off limits to visitors due to the nesting turtles. Other good beaches on the Island of Zakynthos are featured on the pages that follow…

The Beaches, Resorts and Villages of Zakynthos

Banana Beach

We have already come across the mention of this beach on a previous page but the beach is so good I thought I would mention it one more time. This is because Banana Beach is truly a spectacular beach, Banana beach is one of the longest and biggest sandy beaches on the Island of Zakynthos. It is located at Vasilikos (right before Ammos beach). Banana beach has plenty of space for you and your family to swim, find privacy (if you would rather avoid the crowds) and relax on. On the beach you will find a few quieter beach bars to enjoy a relaxing cold drink or for having a snack right on the beach overlooking the crystal clear blue seawater…

The Beaches, Resorts and Villages of Zakynthos

Zakynthos Town Port Resort

The small, port resort that is in Zakynthos Town has made very few concessions to tourism. Rebuilt after the 1953 AD earthquake with a sterile formality, the capital town beach has little charm, despite a magnificent setting in a large bay and the Bochali hills behind. Quake-wrecked Venetian buildings were bulldozed away and replaced by less attractive architecture. The atmosphere improves when you move further into town, especially in the main Solomos Square, thronged by strolling locals and visitors on mid-summer evenings, with a multitude of tavernas and cafes lining the triangular marble-paved piazza. A statue of the Island's favourite son, Dionysius Solomos, dominates the square. As I have mentioned several times before he wrote the Greek national anthem but, although born here, he lived and died on Corfu (I know that I have mentioned this before but it is so significant to the history of Greece I think it is well worth repeating again). Tavernas and shops line the maniacally busy Strada Marina road which is part of the one-way system and is the main traffic route to the towns very busy ferry port…

The Beaches, Resorts and Villages of Zakynthos

Zakynthos Town Port Resort

Zakynthos Town has three interesting museums. The Byzantine Museum, arguably the best, has some 17th century paintings of the Ionian School and some very good icons. The renovated church of Agios Nicholas dates from 1561 and the spectacular Agios Dionysius, often lit up late at night, has a magnificent silver coffin said to house the relics of the island's patron saint. The road north out of Zakynthos Town runs behind the small town beach which is backed by vineyards and fruit orchards…

The Beaches, Resorts and Villages of Zakynthos

Zakynthos Town Port Resort

The long stretch of coast north-west of Zakynthos Town is one of the most commercialised. You will find good, sandy beaches and shallow waters here. This makes it a popular location for family holidays. The whole area is beach fronted by large hotels. This area is a firm favourite with those holidaymaker's that like to do little else during summer Greek Island holidays than soak up the sun, sand, sea and is close to all the other amenities needed for a happy holiday. If you prefer somewhere a bit less crowded than I suggest you look elsewhere on the Island…

The Beaches, Resorts and Villages of Zakynthos

Tsilivi Beach Resort

The resort of Tsilivi is north of Zakynthos Town and is a family friendly resort increasingly favoured by package tour operators. The long, wide beach of golden sand has plenty of sun loungers available and some showers and toilets are also provided. The sea is very shallow and therefore, very safe for children. Heavy winter rains can wash sand away from the western end to reveal rocks and stone; much better sand is to be found at the eastern end of the beach. There are the usual water sports provided here and, being north facing, it can get very windy enough even for wind surfers to let rip. The low dunes and scrub bordering the beach help give Tsilivi beach a wide-open feel…

The Beaches, Resorts and Villages of Zakynthos

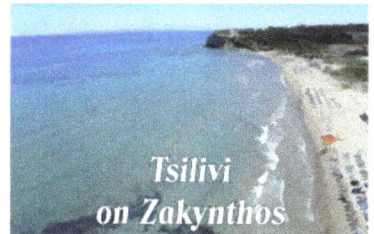 

Tsilivi Beach Resort

Some visitors have, in the past, complained about the amount of litter left on the beach. I recommend that you head to the small cove situated just below the Alexandre Hotel as this part of the beach gets regularly cleaned. The resort of Tsilivi is packed with restaurants, tavernas and menus lean heavily towards burger-Brit tastes. You will also find a chip shop and a McDonald's here. All of the above may not suit all tastes as this resort is a bit like being in a UK resort but with the added benefit of sunshine! There are plenty of family-type entertainment here too such as karaoke bars, crazy golf, and bowling. If you like that sort of thing then Tsilivi is the place for you. The resort of Tsilivi is about 10 km from Zakynthos Airport…

The Beaches, Resorts and Villages of Zakynthos

Tsilivi Beach Resort

Tsilivi Beach Resort has a fine sandy beach and is one of the busiest and liveliest resorts on the Island of Zakynthos. Tsilivi beach is located just 6 km from Zakynthos town. This is a very highly developed tourist resort which makes Tsilivi a favourite destination among young travellers, mixed groups and families alike. The popularity of this resort is largely due to its beautiful surroundings, long sandy beach, ample choice of activities, water sports, local amenities of bars, tavernas, hotels and a very active nightlife scene…

The Beaches, Resorts and Villages of Zakynthos

Tsilivi Beach Resort

Just to the north of Tsilivi on the Island of Zakynthos is a clutch of pretty beaches at Tragaki, Limanaki, Ampoula and Bouka. The main attractions of these beaches are the lovely beach tavernas and happy music bars located there which all help make this area of Zakynthos increasingly popular with families. The proximity of the capital to this area and the regular bus services which run between the resorts and the capital town promises Island visitors a quiet day on the beach soaking up the sun followed by a lively night out in Zakynthos Town…

The Beaches, Resorts and Villages of Zakynthos

Tragaki Beach Resort

The village of Tragaki is built on the side of the Kavelaris hills that are set amongst olive groves and has panoramic views over the bay. We stayed in this resort the last time we visited the Island of Zakynthos at the Louis Plagos Beach Hotel and loved the quality of the hotel, the food and the good service we received from the staff. We went onto Tragaki beach most days during our holiday and enjoyed it very much. Please note that the beach is of pebbles and so beach footwear is not only a great idea but essential. Most holiday accommodation, however, is in nearby Planos which backs onto a beach below Tragaki where there is also a camp site. Nearby the village of Bouka has a long and pleasant stretch of sand with an attractive little fishing harbour at one end where you can enjoy camping close to the seashore on the long, thin sand and pebble beach at Ampoula. The seawater at Ampoula is shallow near the shore, so it is good for children, but be aware there is a steep incline a little way off shore so caution is advised. The beaches on the Island get quieter as you head west. The road to Bouka also leads to the remains of a Venetian observatory, which is well worth a visit. Inland in the village of Sarakinda there is a small water park which is great for the children. Tragaki is about 12 km from Zakynthos Airport…

The Beaches, Resorts and Villages of Zakynthos

Alykanas Beach Resort

The resort at Alykanas sits at the head of the huge sandy bay that sweeps around to the neighbouring resort of Alykes. The soft golden sand shelves gently into the sea and the beach is backed by low dunes, some scrub and several olive groves. The sand narrows and turns to pebble the nearer you get to Alykes. The good facilities and shallow safe seawater makes Alykanas a favourite with families. It is very picturesque and local fishing boats use the small harbour at one end of the beach. A large hotel complex dominates the other end. Bars, tavernas, shops and mini-markets, line the resort's main street. Many restaurants are English-owned, serving up the usual fish and chips and full English breakfast for those who want it…

The Beaches, Resorts and Villages of Zakynthos

Alykanas Beach Resort

The resort of Alykanas has a very relaxed and friendly atmosphere and those who prefer a more lively time can walk along the shore to Alykes in 10 minutes. The popular 'Trainaki' train tour that runs between Alykes and Alykanas takes in the hill village of Katastari, the Vertagias Caves, the folk museum at Pigadakis and the church of Ag. Panteleimona with a snack-refreshment stop at the Kaki Rahi taverna and makes a great day trip out for all the family. Alykanas is about 18 km from Zakynthos Airport…

The Beaches, Resorts and Villages of Zakynthos

Alikanas beach

The Alikanas beach is partly rocky and partly a sandy beach. Extending beyond Alykes and split into two parts by Cape Agia Kyriaki, Alikanas offers white sandy beaches with dunes, a fishing port and local amenities. There is also a picturesque 'mini wreck' of a sunken boat in the sea (reminiscent of the very famous Navagio shipwreck on the island and a must to visit). Alykanas with its shallow, warm seawater makes it an ideal resort for young children and their families to stay in when on the Island of Zakynthos…

The Beaches, Resorts and Villages of Zakynthos

Alykes Beach Resort

Alykes beach is a three kilometers stretch of golden sand that sweeps around the bay from Alykanas and it is said, by many, to be the best beach to be found north of the capital of Zakynthos. Alykes, sometimes spelt Alikes, gets its name from the large, flat salt pans that lie behind the sandy beach situated at the southern end of the resort. It is important for parents of small children to know that the sea bed is very shallow for several metres out into the sea but then it dips sharply away. This makes the beach ideal for children paddling close to the shore, and great for surfers who ride big breakers that are often whipped up by the northerly winds…

The Beaches, Resorts and Villages of Zakynthos

Alykes Beach Resort

The centre of Alykes beach is the busiest spot but those looking for a more peaceful sunbathing location need only walk a short distance in either direction to where the crowds begin to thin out, although it is worth knowing that the pebbles are more prevalent to the east side of the beach. Alykes village is very compact, just a couple of streets with the usual tourist shops, tavernas and cafes. Alykes may be more developed than its neighbour Alykanas but bars are still generally low key and most close around midnight. There is even a tourist train from Alykes to Alykanas. The resort of Alykes is about 17 km from Zakynthos Airport…

The Beaches, Resorts and Villages of Zakynthos

Alykes Beach

Alykes Beach is one of the most popular resorts on the island of Zakynthos. Alykes beach takes its name from the salt flat found in the area. The beach is generally sandy but there are patches of pebbles in some areas on the beach. The municipality of the resort of Alykes has greatly developed the area over recent years and this has now made the resort one of the top holiday seekers destinations on the Island of Zakynthos. It has many excellent hotels to choose from and very good restaurants to enjoy. The open aspect of the sea, in the region, makes it ideal for water sports like wind surfing and water skiing…

The Beaches, Resorts and Villages of Zakynthos

 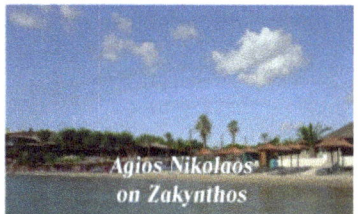

Agios Nikolaos Beach

Beyond Alykes the north coast of the Island of Zakynthos shifts into a long series of cliffs and rock, dotted with small pebble coves, many of them difficult to reach except by boat. The cliffs get wilder and steeper until they reach the tiny port of Agios Nikolaos about 30 km from Zakynthos Town. Do not confuse this resort with the resort of the same name in the south of Zakynthos. This Agios Nikolaos has a small pebble beach and nearby rocky coves found by going off any of the many tracks that snake along the coast. The setting is idyllic, but the buildings around the port are a disappointment. The port has ferry links to Kefalonia and caiques often pull in on their way to visit the famous Blue Caves of Zakynthos. Agios Nikolaos is also a popular mooring point for visiting yachts and boats and a good place to wander off the tourist trail. There are tavernas and cafes in the village and on the coast road so the visitor will not go hungry or thirsty during their stay/visit here…

The Beaches, Resorts and Villages of Zakynthos

 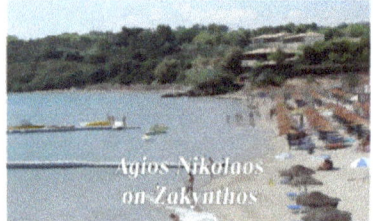

Agios Nikolaos Beach

Agios Nikolaos is a small, attractive stretch of good sand split by an outcrop of rock and crowned by a chapel. It is also a very popular water sports centre. The resort is named after the striking chapel that sits on the bluff above the beach and should not be mistaken for its namesake port in the north-west. There was a fishing port here once but sailing is now pretty much confined to windsurfing, pleasure craft and excursion boats. Agios Nikolaos beach has a wide arc of soft, sand normally packed with sunbeds. It has a scattering of apartments and hotels. The bare landscape around Agios Nikolaos makes it feel rather more remote than it is but things improve inland where there you will find green pine forests and shady olive groves…

The Beaches, Resorts and Villages of Zakynthos

Agios Nikolaos Beach

Is right next to Banana beach at Vasilikos, you will find the sandy beach of Agios Nikolaos (Ammos). This is one of the very best beaches on the Island of Zakynthos. It has perfect fine golden sand, shallow seawater, a number of beach bars (with Wi-Fi), umbrellas, sunbeds and tavernas where you can enjoy cold drinks and good food by the beach with wonderful sea views…

The Beaches, Resorts and Villages of Zakynthos

The Village of Volimes

Volimes is the largest of Zakynthos Island's hill villages, actually a conglomeration of three smaller hamlets, but all within a few minutes' walk of each other. Be prepared for the step back in time that the brochures promise you as each village is a cliché living museum, with some of the best preserved buildings on the Island of Zakynthos that were survivors of the 1953 earthquake. In recent years the road to the village has been improved which has made Volimes a must-see stop for sightseeing coach parties. The villagers take every opportunity to get visitors to part with their hard earned Euros by buying the local embroidery, cheese and the exceptionally good local honey. There is a very pleasant cafe opposite the school. I would strongly recommend that independent visitors try to leave the village before the coach parties arrive as they can flood the place out and turn what was once a very tranquil village into a very busy one very quickly…

The Beaches, Resorts and Villages of Zakynthos

The Resorts on the West Coast of Zakynthos

The west coast of the Island of Zakynthos is as dramatic and solid as the east is plain and soft. As a result, few Zakynthos visitors make their way here. Those that do can enjoy isolated sheer limestone cliffs, sometimes plunging 1,000 feet or more straight into the crystal clear sea. Roads on the west coast are often steep and winding and driving them can be tiring, so trips to this part of the Island are only for the more adventurous holidaymaker…

The Beaches, Resorts and Villages of Zakynthos

Porto Vromi Village

You will be greeted by steep limestone bluffs that rise on each side of a narrow inlet at the small and beautiful, village of Porto Vromi. There is a sheltered harbour here that is flecked with fishing boats bobbing up and down in the blue azure sea. The inlet is tipped by a narrow beach strip of white sand and shingle. Porto Vromi means 'Dirty Port' and the name derives from the natural tar that stains the beach here and there so be careful sunbathing here you could end up very dirty. But this is no real problem for visitors and the flecks of tar are easily avoided. Porto Vromi is far enough off the beaten track to ensure that not many visitors venture here. Above the Porto Vromi harbour is the 15th century monastery of Panagia Anafonitria, noted for its fine frescos. There are regular boat trips from the port. Susie and I went on one such trip when on the Island to visit the nearby Blue Caves of Zakynthos…

The Beaches, Resorts and Villages of Zakynthos

Porto Vromi Beach

Is a small picturesque bay with thick sand, pebbles, rocks and deep sea water that is located in the North-West of the Island of Zakynthos. It is near to the lovely mountainous local villages of Maries, Anafonitria and Orthonies. The cove is full of little caves and has scenic views of the surrounding rocks and cliffs. From here, like us, you can catch a boat to the famous Navagio (Shipwreck) beach. Apart from the odd canteen or beach bar there are not many facilities around Porto Vromi so remember to come prepared with what food and/or drink you may need during you visit to the area…

The Beaches, Resorts and Villages of Zakynthos

The Village of Kampi

High on the western cliffs of Zakynthos perches the village of Kampi. It is unfortunately another target of the day trip coach parties. Cliff top tavernas offer romantic sea views from the 300-metre-high cliffs and many visitors come to watch the sun setting over the waves. Kampi is remote enough to ensure the views can usually be enjoyed in comfort but visitors may be unlucky if their visit coincides with an evening coach party. The tavernas can quickly fill up, especially on the popular Greek nights held regularly for the coach visitors. Kampi village is little more than a cluster of stone-built houses linked by narrow streets. There are however, attractive alternative cafes and tavernas away from the sunset-watching crowds on the cliff top. Kampi village also has a small and interesting folk museum stuffed with domestic and agricultural paraphernalia so why not visit it while you are in the village …

The Beaches, Resorts and Villages of Zakynthos

The Resorts on the South Coast of Zakynthos

The huge sandy bay of Laganas accounts for most of the south coast beach resorts, along with the peninsula at Vassilikos which is characterised by picturesque coves and rich vegetation. Vassilikos has been 'discovered' relatively recently and each year new hotels sprout up to meet the growing demand for accommodation here but the scenery is well worth seeing for those willing to explore this part of the Island of Zakynthos…

The Beaches, Resorts and Villages of Zakynthos

Limni Keriou (Keri) Beach Resort

The resort of Limni Keriou, also called Keri, sits on the southern tip of the Island of Zakynthos on the western side of Laganas Bay. There was a lake here once, now drained, and the area is often referred to as Keri Lake. The steep, narrow beach has more pebbles than sand but it is still very attractive, with warm shallow waters and a small river running into the sea for added interest. The picturesque village has many pre-earthquake buildings and the view from Limni Keriou beach is impressive, with high cliffs flanking both sides and the turtle nesting islet of Marathonisi lying offshore. Paths along the coast that lead to secluded coves and a rough track leads to a cliff top lighthouse where a small car park near the taverna offers spectacular views of the nearby limestone sea arches. Altogether we found it to be a lovely place to visit during our holiday on the Island…

The Beaches, Resorts and Villages of Zakynthos

Limni Keriou (Keri) Beach Resort

In Limni Keriou (Keri) boats can be hired to visit the turtle nesting islet of Marathonisi but ecologists warn that the constant swarms of visitors frighten the shy loggerhead turtles away and fewer nest there each year. Marathonisi has reefs that link it to the cape of Marathias and there are two small beaches on the islet. Turtles nest on a long sand bank and it is a protected part of the marine park but that does not stop turtle watchers scaring the creatures off before they get there. Just inland of Keriou is the pretty village of Lithakia, one of the oldest on the Island of Zakynthos and built on the lower slopes of Megalo Vouno. Lithakia has been little touched by tourism even though it lies between the resorts of Keri Lake and Laganas. The church of Agios Ioannis is a fine example of traditional Zakynthian church architecture and is well worth a visit during your holiday on the Island…

The Beaches, Resorts and Villages of Zakynthos

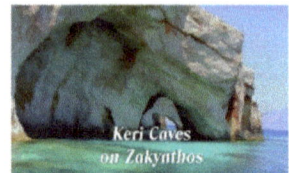 

Keri Caves

Even though it does not qualify as a beach and you can only access it by the sea, Keri Caves is definitely worth visiting. Just off Keri Cape you can find this little paradise of crystal clear turquoise waters and a succession of caves from which the area takes its name. Many divers visit the area as well as visitors on boat trips. The beach is rocky and sensible shoes are a must when visiting this must see location on the Island of Zakynthos. Susie and I enjoyed our visit to the caves very much…

The Beaches, Resorts and Villages of Zakynthos

Keri Beach

Is a mixed sandy and rocky beach. Keri is one of the most scenic destinations on the South of the Island of Zakynthos. It consists of the area formed by Keri Lake, the sea and the traditional village at the top of the hill. Limni Keriou (Keri Lake) took its name from the wetland that surround it and it is still home to many animal and plant species. If you visit Keri beach you will find a narrow strip of seashore and a pedestrianised walkway that runs along the sea front where you will also find local tavernas, cafes and bars…

The Beaches, Resorts and Villages of Zakynthos

Agios Sostis Beach Resort

In recent years the quiet resort of Agios Sostis has attracted holiday development. This was initially done to provide additional accommodation close to the hugely busy and popular resort of Laganas which lies two kilometres around the bay to the east. This pleasant resort has a wide gently shelving sand and pebble beach backed by a couple of tavernas with low cliffs at the southern end where the beach turns to rocks before meeting the wall of the substantial harbour located further beyond…

The Beaches, Resorts and Villages of Zakynthos

Agios Sostis Beach Resort

The beach is named after the chapel on the picturesque islet that sits out in the bay to the south, connected to the resort by a dramatic wooden bridge. The resort is pretty un-commercial so there are no clubs and discos but there is the large Laganas campsite just inland. Tour operators tend to sell Agios Sostis as being livelier than it actually is but Laganas is only a 20-minute walk along a coastal track or five minutes by car or bus. Excursion boats offer turtle spotting trips to the offshore islet of Marathonisi but unfortunately tourists do disturb these very shy creatures so I would not recommend that you go on one! They are seriously disturbed by the daily swarms of day trippers which often results in them failing to lay their eggs. Agios Sostis is about 10 km from Zakynthos International Airport…

The Beaches, Resorts and Villages of Zakynthos

Laganas Beach Resort

Laganas is by far the biggest and most commercialised resort on the Island of Zakynthos, Laganas heaves with bars, cafes and shops for more than a kilometre, all offering an indiscriminate diet of junk food, fry-ups, bargain booze and tacky souvenirs. Laganas is not the ideal place for a peaceful break; they party around the clock here. Evening neon flashes along a Golden Mile of deafening music bars full of 'out for a lark' revelers. There are at least 100 bars on the main Laganas strip and they outnumber restaurants by about ten to one. The beach is the biggest on the island and stretched for nearly nine kilometres. The sands are firm, hard packed where cars roll over them and they are littered with touts plugging the night clubs and flogging things of little or no value…

The Beaches, Resorts and Villages of Zakynthos

Laganas Beach Resort

Despite all the noise, mess and disruption the shallow water makes Laganas beach an ideal beach for both families and for nesting turtles. The meeting of nature and tooth-and-claw businessmen has not been a happy one. Happy to cash in with tacky turtle trinkets and t-shirts, the ruthlessness of the exploitation of the rare turtles is slowly killing them off as nests are bulldozed to make way for sun loungers and glass-bottom boat trips scaring the shy creatures away. Stung by repeated criticism from the Council of Europe, Laganas has at least banned motorised water sports, but protection laws are widely ignored, nesting sites are dug up and the law-breakers go unpunished. As one commentator said "the animal will be killed off, only to live on as a Laganas fridge magnet". Frankly, anyone who cares about nature should avoid Laganas. There are plenty of places to stick a beach brolly other than through a clutch of turtle eggs or preventing them nesting just to get a photo. If you think the comments above are a bit harsh than sorry. For those of you who still want to go here the transfer distance to Laganas is about 8 km from Zakynthos Airport…

The Beaches, Resorts and Villages of Zakynthos

 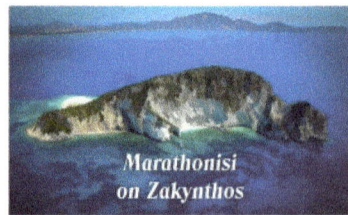

Marathonisi Beach

This little paradise is the islet of Marathonisi and it is situated in Laganas bay. It is a protected wildlife area and part of the National Marine Park. NOTE: Strict visiting and mooring regulations apply. It is worth visiting the sandy beach for a dive into the crystal clear seawater and to admire the beautiful natural heritage of the island. Please respect the local rules and regulations of beaching, anchoring and mooring to help preserve this natural treasure and the turtle nesting sites on the islet…

The Beaches, Resorts and Villages of Zakynthos

Kalamaki Beach Resort

Kalamaki beach resort is basically the upmarket end of Laganas beach, the dark sands of Kalamaki are equal to its neighbour but the atmosphere on the beach is nowhere near as raucous. The sand is soft on the long beach and the water very shallow, with some impressive rock formations along the shore. I have actually stayed in this resort at the Venus Hotel myself on a previous holiday on the Island of Zakynthos and found it to be far less busy and less crowded than Laganas, Kalamaki is a great family beach holiday destination. The resort is enclosed by olive and citrus groves with the backdrop of Mount Skopos in the distance. Although planes fly in low over the beach to land at the nearby airport they are not really a big problem and have become something of a tourist attraction in their own right…

The Beaches, Resorts and Villages of Zakynthos

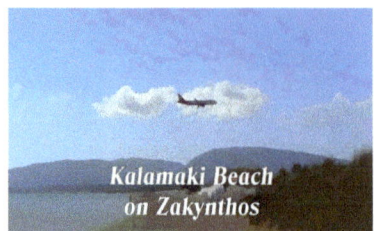

Kalamaki Beach Resort

Kalamaki nightlife mainly consists of touring the local tavernas and bars with those looking for something more lively heading for the bright lights of Laganas just down the coast. Kalamaki beach is also a favourite with the egg-laying turtles and tracks lead down from the village to the protected nesting sites at the back of the beach. Visitors are asked to stick to these designated paths. Wildlife protection is more in evidence here than at nearby Laganas but depressing reports still come in of nest sites being bulldozed or used as illegal waste dumps and urgent steps need to be taken to end this practice. Kalamaki is about 5 km from Zakynthos Airport and therefore, transfer times are very small as a result…

The Beaches, Resorts and Villages of Zakynthos

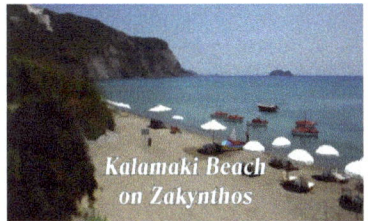

The Venus Hotel…

Kalamaki Beach

This scenic golden sandy beach with warm shallow waters stretches out for approximately 3 km before merging with Laganas and Agios Sostis further on. It is a protected nesting ground for the loggerhead turtle Caretta-Caretta, therefore visitors are not allowed on the beach before sunrise or after sundown to ensure that the turtles are not disturb whilst laying their eggs…

The Beaches, Resorts and Villages of Zakynthos

Vassilikos Peninsula Beach Resort

The maze of unmarked roads that once crisscrossed the Vassiikos peninsula were once a recipe for getting lost but things have improved following an influx of holiday development. Vassilikos has some of the best countryside on the Island of Zakynthos and great beaches too. Tourism used to be upmarket, but big tour companies are gradually taking over, although thankfully its conservation status has stemmed Laganas-like development so far…

The Beaches, Resorts and Villages of Zakynthos

Gerakas Beach Resort

On the eastern side of the peninsula at Gerakas, also spelt Yerakas, is a long, crescent of golden sand and shallow water backed by sandstone cliffs with views across the bay to Laganas. Often voted among one of the best beaches in Europe, Gerakas gets it share of tourists during the day but, being also a major turtle breeding ground, it is off limits from dusk to dawn. Wardens based at the information centre above patrol the nesting areas where sunbathing is banned. There are no water sports and visiting hours are limited. Its conservation area status has spared Gerakas the ugly fate of resorts like Laganas. A trio of tavernas provide the basics and there is car parking near the mini market on the way down to the beach. The cliffs at the southern end of Gerakas turn to white clay that visitors once used as a natural sun block but they are now unsafe and have been closed off following several rock falls. Be warned!…

The Beaches, Resorts and Villages of Zakynthos

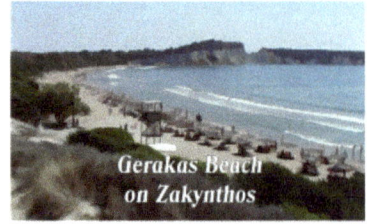 

Gerakas Beach

At the southern-most tip of the Island of Zakynthos you will find the Gerakas peninsula. The sandy beach of Gerakas forms the eastern part of Laganas bay. It is a protected area of the National Marine Park and is a prime nesting ground for the endangered loggerhead turtle Caretta-Caretta. The shallow turquoise seawater combined with the golden sandy beach and the rocky formations in the distance all help to make-up an impressive spectacle and it is therefore, a must see for any Island visitor…

The Beaches, Resorts and Villages of Zakynthos

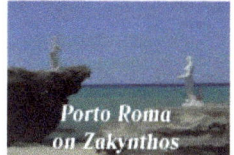 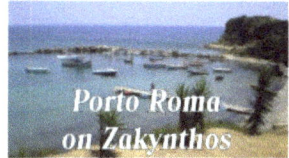

Porto Roma Beach

At the tip of the Gerakas peninsula is the tiny cove of Porto Roma which has a narrow sandy beach with tavernas overlooking the sea. A sublimely beautiful spot with olives and pines touching the shore below cliffs covered in rich vegetation, the beach takes its name from a former Zakynthos notable, Alexandros Romas, who lived here. The waters are shallow and the shore gently shelving and, although remote, the small beach can still fill up quickly with visitors in the high season. Porto Roma has a couple of beach bars, three tavernas and some small shops. Luxury apartments have been built behind the beach but they are not particularly intrusive. This resort is yet another must visit on your holiday to the Paradise Island of Zakynthos…

The Beaches, Resorts and Villages of Zakynthos

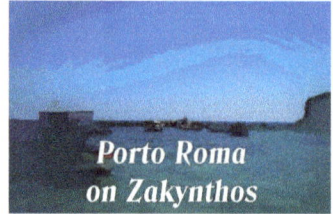 

Porto Roma Beach

Porto Roma beach has a small and peaceful sand-and-pebble beach next to the Gerakas peninsula. Often by-passed in favour of the more well-known Gerakas, Porto Roma has maintained a quiet and picturesque quality which is favoured by families and couples alike. There are a few local amenities around like tavernas, beach bars and small shops for your convenience. A small jetty and fishing port are also an attractive addition to the sightseeing experience when visiting this remarkably beautiful place…

The Beaches, Resorts and Villages of Zakynthos

Vassilikos Beach Resort

The area around Ano Vassilikos is reached by a very scenic drive through pine patterned hills to a tiny hamlet above a narrow beach of sand and pebble. The Island maps are vague on the exact location of Vassilikos village but all the hamlets here come with picturesque bays and coves attached. The main hotel development is confined to the north where the popular Banana Beach owes more to the bulldozer than to nature. The Vassilikos area has long been a nature reserve and efforts have been made to combine tourism and conservation. Water sports, for example, are either banned or sharply curbed. Vassilikos is a quiet resort with entertainment limited to that offered by hotels. For nightlife many head for the clubs and bars of Argassi. Vassilikos beach is about 17 km from Zakynthos Airport…

The Beaches, Resorts and Villages of Zakynthos

Porto Zoro Beach

Porto Zoro is one of the most spectacular beaches on the peninsula and is reached off the main road north out of Vassilikos and before the turn to Argassi. A narrow winding road leads to a small crescent of sharp sand with a clutch of offshore rocks to the east that are ideal for people like me who love to snorkel. The Porto Zoro beach is gently shelving but can be steep near the rock formations where there are plenty of rocks underwater offshore. A hotel is located just behind the beach and sunbeds cram the shoreline and be warned in the evening there is often the loud thump of disco music from the hotel beach bar to disturb the otherwise peaceful evenings…

The Beaches, Resorts and Villages of Zakynthos

Porto Zorro Beach

Is best known for its two picturesque rocky formations emerging from the sea, Porto-Zorro is a well-organised sandy beach with clear clean seawater and easily accessible facilities such as beach bars, tavernas and accommodation. Popular with young tourists, couples and families alike. Ideal for beach bar cocktails, music, leisure and fun for the whole family. So if you like to be in an active and beautiful location than Porto Zorro may be the one for you…

The Beaches, Resorts and Villages of Zakynthos

Argassi Beach Resort

In Argassi beach resort the hotels crawl up the hillside overlooking the shingle beach at Argassi, so narrow in places that visitors are hard put to lie down without getting their feet wet. The water is very shallow for many metres out to sea making Argassi a safe beach for children. Note beyond the shingle shore it is sandy underfoot. Argassi is a popular family resort with a good selection of shops and tavernas. Argassi hotels opt for family rooms and there is lots to occupy the children, from mini golf to a small farm. Smarter hotels hug the shore intertwined with tavernas and bars, although greater choice can be found in Zakynthos Town which is only three kilo-metres north from the resort. Argassi is about 6 km from Zakynthos Airport…

The Beaches, Resorts and Villages of Zakynthos

Porto Roxa Beach

As with Limnionas, the small cove at Porto Roxa is a secluded beach tucked away from the busy commercialised tourist areas on the island. The beach is a mix of sand and rocks. Its deep azure crystal clear seawater are a refreshing break from the heat of the beach in the peak months of summer, however remember to take some food and drink with you when you visit this beach as there are not many facilities near-by. In the rocks, there is, a spring board for the experienced swimmers to dive straight into the inviting blue/green seawater. Alternatively, you can follow the steep path down to the seawater edge and go into the sea from there…

The Beaches, Resorts and Villages of Zakynthos

Porto Koukla Beach

This small sandy beach is a few kilometers away from busy Laganas. It has many local amenities. Porto Koukla beach is a favourite destination with families and groups. There are plenty of waterfront fish tavernas to choose from after a refreshing swim. This is a great alternative beach for those staying in Laganas or the nearby camp site…

The Beaches, Resorts and Villages of Zakynthos

 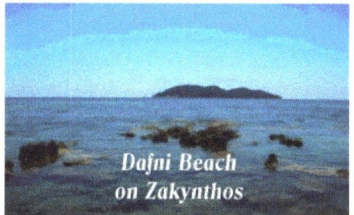

Dafni Beach

Is a mix of rocks and sand. It is one of the most beautiful beaches on the island with mesmerizing views of Pelouzo in the distance (a protected islet not accessible to visitors), Dafni is part of the National Marine Park therefore visiting restrictions apply. This is yet another must visit place to see during your stay on the Island of Zakynthos…

The Beaches, Resorts and Villages of Zakynthos

 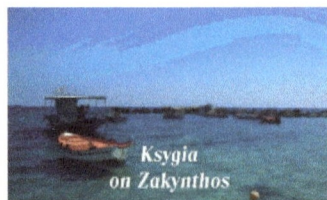

Ksygia Beach

Ksygia beach is a small pebbly-rocky beach that is approximately 20 km from Zakynthos Town. The beach is known for its underwater Sulphur spring which also gives a distinctive smell to the area. The locals are convinced of the water's remedial qualities, especially for conditions such as arthritis. If you are a sufferer, like me, a visit to Ksygia beach during your holiday may prove very worthwhile indeed!…

The Beaches, Resorts and Villages of Zakynthos

Marathias Beach

Is a beautiful white pebbly-rocky beach that is located opposite Marathonissi islet at Keri Lake. To access the beach you need to drive up the hill and park off the main road before you then have to walk down a steep path which leads to the sea. Its secluded location provides a relaxing and peaceful setting but even though it is never over crowded it is becoming very popular with well-informed visitors so my advice is to get there early…

The Beaches, Resorts and Villages of Zakynthos

Makris Gialos Beach

Makris Gialos is a beautiful sandy-pebbly beach with deep, cool crystal clear seawater in the north of the Island of Zakynthos. This is a great destination to head for after a car tour of the northern part of the Island as we did when we were on the island. The crystal clear seawater and small caves found in the little bay are perfect for snorkeling and exploration. Adults and children alike will enjoy their visit here very much…

The Beaches, Resorts and Villages of Zakynthos

Porto Limnionas Beach

Is a rocky beach and is on the west side of the Island of Zakynthos, approximately 7 km from Agios Leon, you will find Porto Limnionas a beautiful cove tacked away from the busy tourist resorts however, there is no beach as such and in order to approach the seawater you will need to walk down steep steps formed in the rocks. The refreshing cold seawater that awaits you there are a combination of sea currents and underwater streams. We found it a lovely place to spend some time swimming in the sea during our holiday to the island…

The Beaches, Resorts and Villages of Zakynthos

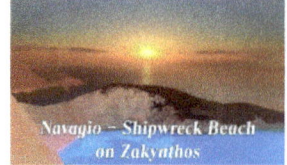 

The World Famous Navagio (or Shipwreck Bay) Beach

Navagio is a rocky beach and home to a world famous shipwreck. We went there, like so many others, during our last holiday to the Island and like so many others we just had to write our names on the hull of the shipwrecked boat. In 1983 an illegal boat carrying cigarettes was washed up onto the shore of the Agios Georgios bay, as it was then known and has stayed there ever since. This is one of the most photographed beaches (wrecks) in Europe. Note the beach can only be reached by boat. The beach is located on the west coast of the Island of Zakynthos under the famous and picturesque mountainous village of Volimes. The beach and village are another holiday must visit locations on the island of Zakynthos…

The Beaches, Resorts and Villages of Zakynthos

Before we move on we will look at some of my artwork images of the beautiful beaches, resorts and villages that can be found on the Island of Zakynthos…

The Beaches, Resorts and Villages of Zakynthos

Above are more of my artwork pictures of the beautiful beaches on the Greek Paradise Island of Zakynthos…

The Beaches, Resorts and Villages of Zakynthos

Above are more of my artwork pictures of the beautiful beaches on the Greek Paradise Island of Zakynthos…

The Beaches, Resorts and Villages of Zakynthos

Above are more of my artwork pictures of the beautiful beaches on the Greek Paradise Island of Zakynthos…

The Beaches, Resorts and Villages of Zakynthos

Above are more of my artwork pictures of a beautiful sea rock formation and of Keriou beach on the Greek Paradise Island of Zakynthos…

The Beaches, Resorts and Villages of Zakynthos

Above are more of my artwork pictures of just two of the many beautiful views that await you on the Greek Paradise Island of Zakynthos…

The Beaches, Resorts and Villages of Zakynthos

Above are more of my artwork pictures of the beautiful Greek Paradise Island of Zakynthos…

The Beaches, Resorts and Villages of Zakynthos

Just before we leave this chapter, and move on to the next chapter, which focuses on our own holiday experiences when visiting the Island of Zakynthos, we will enjoy just a few more artwork pictures of the beautiful Greek Paradise Island of Zakynthos…

In the next chapter we will read about and see images taken on our most recent holiday to the Island of Zakynthos. So if you are ready please turn the page and join Susie, Ginny and me on our holiday to the paradise Greek holiday island of Zakynthos…

Our Holiday to Zakynthos

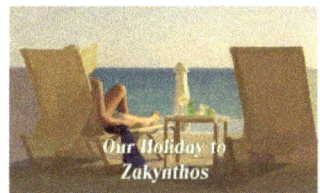

Venus Hotel…

Navagio Beach…

We have holidayed on the Island of Zakynthos twice in the recent past. The first time was at the Venus Hotel in the resort of Kalamaki. The hotel was lovely and it was just a short stroll down a narrow lane to the beautiful sandy beach of Kalamaki. The beach is used by the Loggerhead Turtles (Caretta–Caretta) to lay their eggs on at night so you had to be careful not to disturb them and to keep well away from the beach from dusk till dawn. We visited the resort of Laganas and many other beaches, resorts and villages whilst we were on the Island. We also enjoyed several boat trips as well including going to Navagio beach (shipwreck beach) like so many others it seemed because the beach was so full of people even though it could only be reached by boat…

Our Holiday to Zakynthos

The second, and more recent time that we visited the Island along with our daughter Ginny, we stayed at the Iberostar Plagos Beach Hotel (see above) near Tragaki. This was the best and most luxurious hotel we have ever stayed in. The hotel food was superb and the hotel pool was lovely, clean and refreshing. Our apartment fronted onto the sea so the sea views from our balcony were spectacular. On several days we went down to the nearby beach which was of pebbles so we bought some beach shoes to wear. Ginny used her underwater camera to take some interesting pictures whilst swimming offshore of our hotel. We once again visited many of the other beaches, resorts and villages on the Island. We also enjoyed several more boat trips as well including going back to Navagio beach (shipwreck beach) like so many others it seemed because the beach was still full even though it could only be reached by boat. Ginny wrote her name on the shipwreck hull just as we had done when we visited the beach during a previous holiday to the Island…

Our Holiday to Zakynthos

Pictures of the Iberostar Plagos Beach Hotel lounge and us in the hotel on the island of Zakynthos…

Our Holiday to Zakynthos

Alan and Susie on a boat trip

Susie and |Ginny on Tragaki beach

Images and artwork re-produced from our holiday photographs taken whilst we were staying at the Iberostar Plagos Beach Hotel on the paradise Greek island of Zakynthos…

Our Holiday to Zakynthos

Images and artwork re-produced from our holiday photographs taken whilst we were staying at the Iberostar Plagos Beach Hotel on the paradise Greek island of Zakynthos…

Our Holiday to Zakynthos

Images and artwork re-produced from our holiday photographs taken whilst we were staying at the Iberostar Plagos Beach Hotel on the paradise Greek island of Zakynthos…

Our Holiday to Zakynthos

One day during our holiday, Susie took our daughter Ginny horse riding during our stay at the Louis Plagos Hotel in Tragaki. I also went with them but did not ride out with them but stayed instead at the stables and enjoyed a few cold drinks, some snacks and a chat with the owner while waiting for their return. We also all went on several day trips out to the main town of Zakynthos, other beach resorts on the Island and on a boat trip around the island. We had some lovely days on the beach just down from our hotel. The beach was very stony but fortunately a shop near-by sold special beach shoes which we used all the time on the beach and in the sea. They were great. On the beach there was a raised grass area where you could sunbathe off the pebbles. There was also a very good small taverna on this grass area where we had our lunches when on the beach. It was great to sit and eat great local sea food while looking out to sea…

Our Holiday to Zakynthos

As I have already mentioned on one day of our holiday we went on an organised coach trip from our hotel into the countryside around us and into the mountains to visit some lovely villages. We were out all day and had our lunch at a taverna that sat atop of a mountain with superb views of the rocky cliffs and sea beyond. The coach trip also included another boat trip to visit the smugglers cove (Navagio Beach or Shipwreck Beach) to see the Island most famous ship wreck. Although we had already visited the wreck once already during this holiday we decided, that as we had paid, we would go again and enjoy what is a splendid location again. Ginny wrote her name on the shipwreck hull, once more, before we all sunbathed for a while on the stony beach. On the small boat back from the shipwreck to the drop off point we were shown "the face of Poseidon" which is a rock formation on the coast that surprisingly did look like a man rising from the sea. Once safely back on dry land we had an evening meal at a local taverna watching a fabulous sunset before returning to our hotel exhausted but very happy…

Our Holiday to Zakynthos

Later during our holiday, Susie, Ginny and I left our hotel early one morning and went on a turtle island boat cruise that left from a port near Laganas. The boat trip organises said they hoped to show us the famous endangered loggerhead turtles swimming just offshore as well as the sights and sounds of the Island of Zakynthos from the sea. We sailed around the peninsula to the island of Marathonisi, which is also known as Turtle Island. We did get to see a turtle swimming in the sea which was great. The boat stopped several times during the trip so that Ginny and I, and the other passengers who wanted to, could enjoyed ourselves swimming in the clear blue sea before we continued onto the caves of Keri before returning to the dock and back to the hotel. At the end of our holiday we all said how much we had enjoyed our stay on the Paradise Island of Zakynthos. So now that I have shared with you our experiences of holidaying on the Island of Zakynthos it is now time, in the last chapter, for us to explore this Island in wonderful colour images…

Zakynthos in Colour

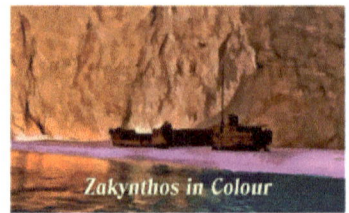
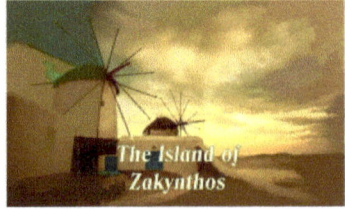

The Venus hotel in Kalamaki and sea view at Keri on the island of Zakynthos

Zakynthos in Colour

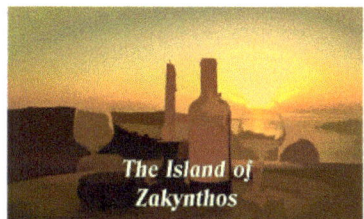

Marathias and boats at Porto Roxa on the island of Zakynthos

Zakynthos in Colour

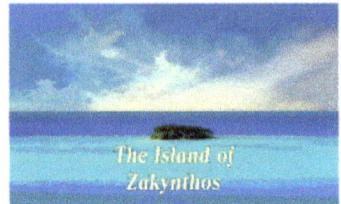

Agios Nikolaos and Argassi on the island of Zakynthos

Zakynthos in Colour

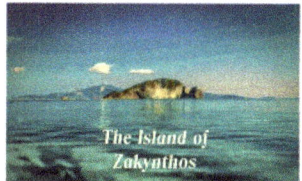 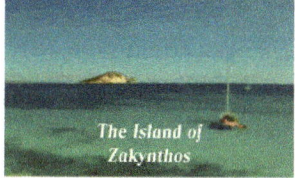

Laganas beach and boat at Limni Keriou on the island of Zakynthos

Zakynthos in Colour

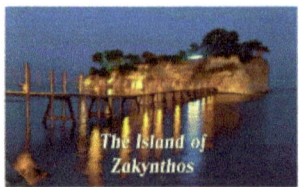

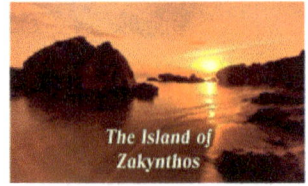

Banana beach and boats at shipwreck beach on the island of Zakynthos

Zakynthos in Colour

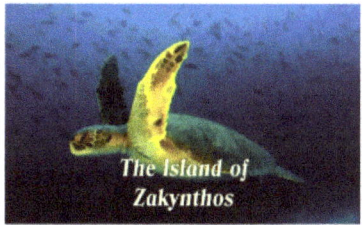

Dafni beach and boat at Marathonisi on the island of Zakynthos

Zakynthos in Colour

Kalamaki beach and view at Kampi on the island of Zakynthos

Zakynthos in Colour

Keri and boats at Ksygia on the island of Zakynthos

Zakynthos in Colour

Marathonisi beach and Laganas beach on the island of Zakynthos

Zakynthos in Colour

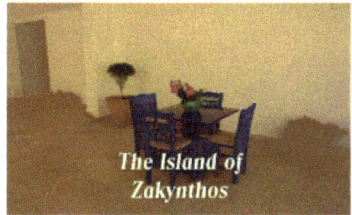

Limni Keriou and drinks at Makris Gialos on the island of Zakynthos

Zakynthos in Colour

 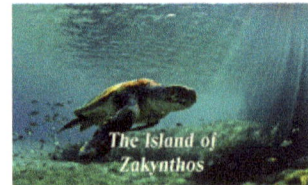

Marathonisi and Banana beach on the island of Zakynthos

Zakynthos in Colour

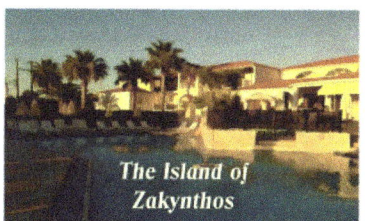

Seats at Volimes and shipwreck beach on the island of Zakynthos

Zakynthos in Colour

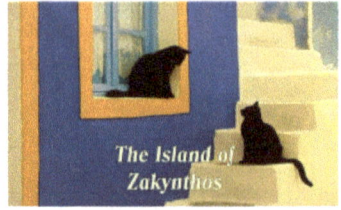
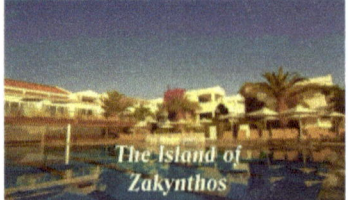

Keri beach and Porto Limnionas on the island of Zakynthos

Zakynthos in Colour

Marathias and boats at Porto Roxa on the island of Zakynthos

Zakynthos in Colour

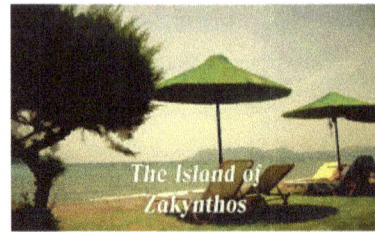 

Banana and Marathias beach on the island of Zakynthos

Zakynthos in Colour

Kalamaki and Marathias beach on the island of Zakynthos

Zakynthos in Colour

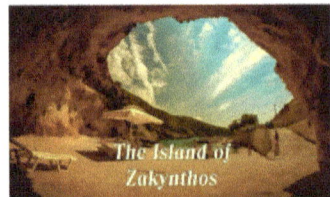

Laganas and Porto Vromi beach on the island of Zakynthos

Zakynthos in Colour

Pictures of the very beautiful Paradise Island of Zakynthos

Sad to say that we have come to the end of this the final chapter of my book so it is time for us to say farewell. Having shared with you some of the Islands history, geography, useful information, resorts, villages, beaches, our holiday experiences and the Greek Paradise Island of Zakynthos in colour, it is therefore, now time to say goodbye. I hope that you have enjoyed our journey of discovery together around this very beautiful Mediterranean Island Paradise. I hope that you will also get to enjoy the Island for yourselves, real soon, and visit for yourselves the Paradise Island of Zakynthos. So it's goodbye from Susie and it's goodbye from me until the next time Happy Holidays…

Acknowledgement

I would like to thank all of the Zakynthian people of Greece that Susie and I met during our holidays on their beautiful Island.

I would also like to thank my publishers Rainbow Publications UK. For publishing this book. Finally I wish to thank my wife Susie for being there for me, her love and the support that she gives me in all that I do everyday of my life.

Susie… 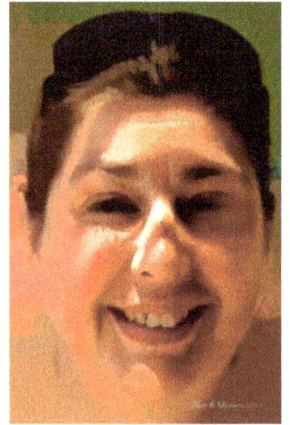  **Alan…**

Copyright © 2020 Alan R. Massen

We wish you all a very special
Thank You

www.ingramcontent.com/pod-product-compliance
Lightning Source LLC
Chambersburg PA
CBHW061928290426
44113CB00024B/2838